PRAISE FOR GAS FIRE HEAT

At Traeger, we embrace a mission to bring people together to create a more flavorful world. Chef Aly's book exemplifies this mission through her unwavering passion for teaching people to cook outdoors, be it crafting quick-and-easy weeknight meals or going all out with a low-and-slow BBQ feast for family and friends. She not only presents an array of techniques and flavors, but also demonstrates that there's no limit to what you can create outdoors.

Jeremy Andrus, CEO of Traeger Grills

Chef Aly Romero has been a treasured Hestan Brand Ambassador and friend for many years. We met Aly as a member of our Hestan Wine Club when she attended our Harvest Party—instantly we felt her passion for sharing her love of cooking and we knew we had to collaborate with her on Hestan. Chef Aly's style is elevated yet approachable and her flavorful recipes and stunning content have been invaluable to the Hestan community. We know *Gas Fire Heat* will inspire others to test her recipes for themselves, embracing her creative flavors and techniques to create memorable meals for family and friends.

Pamela Stafford, Managing Director of Hestan Culinary

Aly is one of the most talented chefs that I have the pleasure of knowing and working alongside. In her new cookbook *Gas Fire Heat* Aly draws from her diverse culinary influences to deliver innovative recipes that can be enjoyed outside with family and friends. Her recipes go beyond traditional BBQ. She has taken many dishes that folks would have traditionally cooked indoors to the outdoors where I believe everything tastes better. The recipes in this cookbook are creative yet approachable and delicious!

Matt Pittman, CEO and Founder of Meat Church

GAS
FIRE
HEAT

Published by Familius LLC, www.familius.com
PO Box 1249, Reedley, CA 93654

Familius books are available at special discounts for bulk purchases, whether for sales promotions or for family or corporate use. For more information, contact Familius Sales at orders@familius.com.

Library of Congress Control Number: 2023950819

Print ISBN 9781641709101
EPUB ISBN 9781641708449
Kindle ISBN 9781641708432
Fixed PDF ISBN 9781641708425

Printed in China

Edited by Peg Sandkam and Abby Tree
Cover design by Brooke Jorden
Book design by Brooke Jorden and Maggie Wickes

10 9 8 7 6 5 4 3 2 1

First Edition

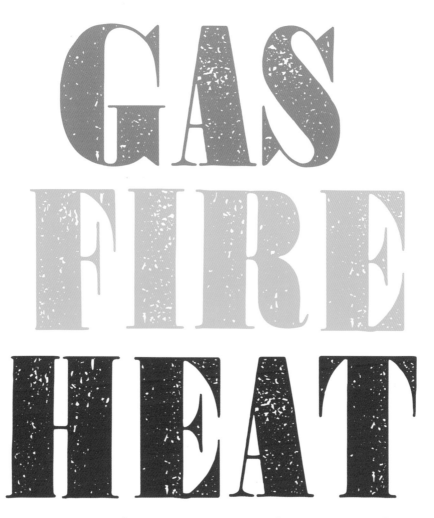

GAS FIRE HEAT

Essential Recipes and Secrets for
COOKING OUTDOORS

ALY ROMERO

TRAEGER AMBASSADOR

This cookbook is dedicated to my family; without them to cook for, I would not be the chef I am today. To my amazing husband, James, who has always encouraged and supported me chasing my dreams and who is my self-proclaimed "biggest fan," as I am of him. And to our three kids—Madi, Nick, and Austin—who I love with all my heart, I am so thankful you have always given me honest feedback about my cooking over the years, and it's my hope you'll always want to come home for dinner! All your varied culinary preferences have challenged me to become better, and your appreciation for the meals I create is what inspires me daily to keep on keeping on. You are my reason, and you fuel my passion to cook!

In loving memory of my mom and dad, who showed me how to lead a life with inner drive, perseverance, and a love of cooking to make my dream a reality.

CONTENTS

INTRODUCTION

HELLO!

I'm Aly Romero, private chef, brand ambassador, media personality, and now officially a cookbook author—but you can just think of me as your friend who cooks!

I've always loved food, not just for its capacity to nourish and sustain us but for its power to comfort and connect us. Across the world's various cultures, food is a fundamental part of our traditions, celebrations, and milestones. Learning about, preparing, and sharing food with others is one of my greatest passions, and that's why I started my food blog back in 2016. That blog led to my success as a brand ambassador, my career as a private chef, and my appearance on *Good Morning America*, *The Chew*, and *Food Network* (I'm still pinching myself!).

It's my great pleasure to welcome you to my very first cookbook, where you can find BBQ, smoking, and grilling recipes as well as some of my favorite tips for having more fun and feeling more confident while cooking outdoors! This book includes all my outdoor favorites, but it also proves that anything you can cook inside, you can cook outside! Each of these recipes can be cooked inside on a rainy day if you just don't feel like heading out to the grill, griddle, or smoker. This cookbook looks at the world of BBQ through a culinary lens and takes it beyond BBQ chicken and ribs (But don't worry, those are still included too!). There's nothing that brings me more joy than helping others prepare and share food with the people they love. So let's get cooking!

BIOGRAPHY

My culinary journey started soon after college and was inspired by my dad, who used to visit from New Zealand for a few months at a time. First thing every morning he would ask me, "What's for dinner tonight, Aly?" I would look at him like he was crazy; it was only 8 a.m., and I hadn't even finished my first cup of coffee! But at night, we would have a glass of wine and cook together, and I soon found that I, too, woke up thinking about dinner. It wasn't simply cooking dinner; it was an experience. I lost my dad in 2013, but I still feel close to him when I cook. In the mornings, my oldest son asks, "Mom, what's for dinner tonight?" and I can't help but smile and think of my dad.

I started my food blog in 2016 when I started culinary school to share some of my twenty-plus years of cooking experience and what I was learning in my culinary classes. For me, food and cooking became an obsession; I wanted to continue learning, growing, and searching for new ways to adapt and elevate everyday recipes with fresh takes and diverse influences.

I was born in New Zealand. Then, as a young child, I lived in Hawaii for seven years, followed by California for most of my high school, college, and adult life. My husband is Greek and Spanish, and we now reside in the Dallas–Fort Worth area of Texas with our three amazing kids. In this cookbook, you will notice the various culinary influences of places my family has lived and ingredients from our diverse backgrounds, which have all shaped and influenced me to become the chef I am today! I love exploring different types of cuisines and incorporating the ingredients and techniques of various flavor profiles. All of it reminds me of "home."

What I love most about food is its power to build community and to help connect us to each other and to our past. Sharing my recipes and experiences through my website has allowed me to discover and contribute to a larger community, which has led to some truly amazing opportunities. In 2018, I was featured on the "You on *The Chew*" recipe showdown and was thrilled when my recipe won. Watching Chef Michael Symon take a bite of my Carnitas Street Tacos and gush over their flavor was a pretty exciting moment! Later that year, a photo of the same recipe was featured on *Good Morning America* in a segment with Gordon Ramsay.

Not long after, I was invited by *Good Morning America* to compete with my husband in a live segment promoting Ayesha Curry's new show, *Family Food Fight*. We made my Apple Cider–Brined Pork Tenderloin with Mango Salsa (see page 61); I was so excited when we brought home the trophy! After the show, the producer asked if we wanted to take the trophy with us and we said, "Yes! Of course!" without hesitation. It was about twenty-four inches tall with all kinds of veggies spewing out of the top. Boy, did we get some looks walking with it through the JFK airport—a definite conversation starter to say the least!

In February 2020, I got a call I had always dreamed of! A casting producer from Food Network called to let me know that our team had been cast for Season 13 of the *Great Food Truck Race*. We were just days away from finding out where we would be going to film the show and then the pandemic hit. Needless to say, everything came to a screeching halt and the filming was put on hold until further notice. My heart sank, I had no idea if that opportunity would ever become a reality. About 8 months later, my phone rang and it was the same producer, filming was back on and she wanted to know if our team was still interested and available to compete on the show. Without hesitation, I said "Yes, of course!". As it turned out, they were casting for 2 seasons and she asked if we would prefer to go somewhere warm or cold. I responded "Definitely somewhere warm!". We were then cast to compete on the season in Alaska...in November! It was the coldest I've ever been in my entire life and we were all definitely unprepared for cooking in the freezing elements. Aside from the cold, competing as the Meatball Mamas on the Great Food Truck Race in Alaska was one of the most amazing experiences of my life and I'm so grateful that we got to go! It was a part of my culinary journey I'll never forget!

It's all been such a fun and crazy ride, and I'm so grateful to be able to share these experiences with my husband and children. As a mom, I've always hoped to inspire my kids to work hard and follow their dreams, whatever they may be!

I lost my mom in February 2022; it was sudden and an utter shock. It was a horrible feeling I'll never forget. Growing up, she was not a "foodie nerd" like my dad was, but she instilled drive in me like no other. She traveled with my brother and me, introduced us to cultures all over the world, and always practiced the motto of "Where there is a will, there is a way." My passion and drive in the culinary space is attributed to her as a role model in my life: a single mom and a complete go-getter. She didn't let anyone tell her she couldn't do something; she just found a way to get it done. As my husband summarized perfectly to me once, I am the exact culmination of both my mom and dad.

I currently work as a private chef, and I've had the honor of cooking for professional athletes and government officials, specializing in dinner parties for events and occasions like milestone birthdays, holiday celebrations, corporate events, and school auctions. Because I'm always striving to learn and create, I love the challenge of innovating new dishes, and preparing classic favorites in unexpected ways.

My involvement with organizations that give back to the community is especially important to me, and for many years I have hosted an annual Friendsgiving to benefit the No Kid Hungry campaign. I've also been a culinary volunteer with World Central Kitchen, helping to feed fire victims, evacuees, and first responders during the fires in Napa, California. During the COVID-19 pandemic, I was invited to contribute an original recipe to *The Quarantine Collective*, an e-cookbook developed by the producers of the *Today Show*. All profits went to benefit the James Beard Foundation's Open for Good campaign to help independent restaurants rebuild after the pandemic.

My husband travels a lot for work, and now that we have three teenagers, there's never a dull moment! Across all of our schedules, life can get pretty chaotic. But no matter how crazy life gets, we always make time to sit down and enjoy dinner together at the end of the day. Sharing fresh, incredible food with the people I love is one of the truest joys of my life and has kept our college-aged daughter coming home for dinner with friends every once in a while. One of my very favorite questions will always be, "Mom, what's for dinner?"

KITCHEN ESSENTIALS/FAVORITE TOOLS

Throughout my culinary career, I've compiled a list of my favorite kitchen tools that help the cooking, grilling, and smoking processes run a lot smoother. Here is a list of some of my favorite grilling tools, including brand preferences that are high quality, durable, and—the biggest key— easy to clean!

Hestan NanoBond skillet: Stainless steel cookware that can be used on a smoker or grill, withstands up to 1050 degrees, and cleans up like new! Lifetime guarantee and well worth the investment.

Traeger smoker: I have owned a few Traegers, and my favorite is the redesigned Ironwood XL.

Burch Barrel grill and smoker: Live-fire cooking over lump charcoal is so much fun on the Burch Barrel! You can lower and raise the grates for direct or indirect cooking.

Lodge cast-iron pans, skillets, large Dutch ovens, and casserole pans: All these cookware pieces can be used on the grill or smoker!

Vertical skewer/spit: Great for making al pastor or gyros at home on the grill or smoker.

Meater probe: My favorite wireless thermometer for outdoor cooking.

Meat Church rubs: My go-to BBQ rubs!

Anova sous vide: My favorite sous vide circulator. I have a few of them and have used them for years with foolproof results.

Vitamix blender: As far as quality high-speed blenders for soups, sauces, and marinades go, the Vitamix is the best!

High-quality baking sheets: I recommend Hestan Culinary here again because they won't warp with high heat.

FoodSaver vacuum sealer: You can use a vacuum sealer for sous vide cooking or to freeze extra meat.

Other small kitchen tools:
- Microplane
- Bench scraper
- Lemon squeezer
- High-quality chef's knife
- Wood cutting board and a plastic one (for raw meat) that can go in the dishwasher
- Metal tongs
- Heat-proof oven mitt for grilling over hot flames
- Mixing bowls and serving platters
- Kitchen shears
- Stasher reusable silicone bags for sous vide cooking

For more information as well as discount codes, check out my Brand Ambassador page.

APPETIZERS

PASTRY-WRAPPED BRIE WITH ROASTED GRAPES

If you've never had roasted grapes, now is your chance! The sweet flavor is intensified and roasting them in a skillet with the pastry-wrapped Brie allows all the flavors to flow together. Pour yourself a glass of wine and dig in!

2 1/2 tablespoons plus 1 teaspoon extra virgin olive oil, divided

1 sheet pastry dough, such as Dufour

8 ounces Brie

Egg wash (one egg beaten with 1 tablespoon water)

1 small bunch of purple, seedless grapes

1/2 teaspoon kosher salt, divided

1 baguette, sliced into 1/2-inch crostini

1/4 teaspoon black pepper

1 tablespoon honey, for drizzle garnish (Manuka is my favorite)

1 teaspoon fresh thyme, for garnish

1–2 tablespoons candied pecans, for garnish

1. Drizzle a 10-inch stainless steel or cast-iron skillet with 1/2 tablespoon olive oil and use a paper towel to spread it around the bottom of the pan.

2. Preheat the grill to medium heat, or about 400 degrees.

3. Trim the pastry dough into a square shape and place the Brie in the center. Wrap the sides of the pastry up around the Brie so every side is sealed. Place in the pan seam-side down and score the top of the pastry, pushing slightly through the rind of the Brie in a pinwheel. Brush the top and sides with egg wash.

4. Place grapes along the side of the pan, leaving a little space between the pastry dough so they're not touching. Drizzle grapes with 1 teaspoon olive oil, and sprinkle 1/4 teaspoon salt over the grapes and puff pastry.

5. Place the skillet on the grill and close the lid. Cook until the puff pastry is golden brown, about 20–25 minutes.

6. While the Brie is cooking, drizzle the crostini with 2 tablespoons olive oil and sprinkle with 1/4 teaspoon salt and pepper.

7. Place the crostini along the side of the grill, toasting a few minutes per side until golden brown; remove to a plate.

8. To serve, use a large spoon to pull apart the puff pastry and allow the cheese to run. Top with a drizzle of honey, thyme, and candied pecans and serve with crostini.

SEARED AHI POKE

Serves 6–8
Prep Time: 5 minutes
Marinade Time: 30 minutes
Cook Time: 15 minutes
Total Time: 50 minutes

A fusion of two of my favorite things—ahi poke and seared ahi—this Seared Ahi Poke has all my favorite flavors in one bite! Avocado also makes a great addition!

1 tablespoon toasted sesame seeds
1 tablespoon black sesame seeds
6 ounces sushi-grade ahi tuna

1 tablespoon extra virgin olive oil
1/3 sweet yellow onion
1 small Persian cucumber, peeled

SAUCE
1/4 cup soy sauce
1 teaspoon fresh ginger, grated
1/2 tablespoon spicy chili crisp

1 tablespoon sesame oil
1 teaspoon furikake seasoning (optional)
2–3 tablespoons vegetable oil

WONTON CHIPS
Vegetable oil
Wonton wrappers, diagonally cut into fourths
Micro greens, for garnish (optional)

Hijiki strands, for garnish (optional)
Crispy fried garlic, for garnish (optional; see page 138)

1. Combine the toasted and black sesame seeds in a small bowl.

2. Pat the tuna with paper towels and drizzle olive oil on all sides. Roll in the sesame seed combo and place uncovered in the refrigerator for 30 minutes.

3. Thinly slice the onion and quarter and dice the cucumber. Set aside.

4. Whisk together the sauce ingredients in a small bowl. Set aside.

5. Heat a flat top grill to high and add 2–3 tablespoons vegetable oil. When hot, remove the tuna from the refrigerator and sear 90 seconds. Then flip and sear 60 seconds. Remove and let rest before slicing.

6. Thinly slice the tuna against the grain into strips and then small chunks.

7. In a large skillet, heat to medium-high heat and add vegetable oil about 1/4-inch deep. When it's hot, add the wonton wrappers to fry until golden brown, flipping halfway, about 2 minutes total cooking time. Strain on a paper towel–lined plate.

8. Add sesame-crusted seared ahi tuna to a bowl along with the onions, cucumbers, and micro greens. Toss gently in the sauce.

9. Top with dried hijiki strands and fried garlic. Serve with wonton chips.

SMOKED BUFFALO CHICKEN DIP

This is a great dip to bring next time you're asked to bring something to share at a party—it's super addicting! Greek yogurt makes it a lighter version without skimping on flavor!

2 cups shredded chicken (rotisserie works great)
1/2 tablespoon granulated garlic
1/2 tablespoon onion powder
1/2 tablespoon smoked paprika
1 tablespoon dried parsley
1/2 teaspoon black pepper
3/4 cup Frank's RedHot Buffalo Wings Hot Sauce (or your favorite brand)
1/2 cup plain, whole milk Greek yogurt

1 cup cream cheese, at room temperature
1/3 cup blue cheese crumbles
1 cup (4 ounces) mozzarella, shredded, divided
1 cup (4 ounces) sharp cheddar, shredded, divided
3 scallions, sliced, reserve dark green parts for garnish
Tortilla chips, for serving

1. Preheat smoker to 375 degrees.

2. In a large bowl, stir together chicken, granulated garlic, onion powder, paprika, parsley, and pepper.

3. Add hot sauce, yogurt, cream cheese, blue cheese, 1/2 cup mozzarella, and 1/2 cup cheddar. Add white and light green scallions. Stir to combine.

4. Pour into a skillet. Sprinkle with another 1/2 cup mozzarella and 1/2 cup cheddar.

5. Smoke for 25–30 minutes, until cheese is melted and bubbly. Rotate skillet halfway through.

6. Sprinkle with remaining scallions and serve with tortilla chips.

PRO TIPS:

- This recipe can also be made in the oven; bake it on the top rack.
- You can substitute Monterey Jack for mozzarella.
- For best results, always shred your own cheese from a block.

GARLIC BUTTER MONKEY BREAD WITH MARINARA

Serves 6–8
Prep Time: 10 minutes
Cook Time: 50 minutes
Total Time: 1 hour

I saw a ton of recipes floating around social media for making sweet monkey bread on the smoker, so I decided to create my own savory version. This Garlic Butter Monkey Bread with Marinara is gone in seconds!

8 tablespoons salted butter

2 cloves of garlic, minced

8 ounces Homemade Marinara (see page 149)

2 cans (13.8 ounces each) pizza dough

6 ounces shredded mozzarella, divided

1 teaspoon chopped fresh basil, for garnish

1 teaspoon chopped fresh parsley, for garnish

1 tablespoon grated fresh Parmesan, for garnish

1. Preheat smoker to 350 degrees.

2. In a small saucepan, add butter and garlic. Once the butter is melted, turn off the heat.

3. Heat the marinara sauce in a saucepan on the stove over medium-low heat.

4. While the marinara heats up, brush 1/4 of the garlic butter around all sides and the center of a Bundt pan.

5. Unroll pizza dough and cut five vertical and four horizontal lines to make twenty equal pieces. Roll each piece into a ball.

6. Create a single layer of rolled pizza dough balls in the Bundt pan. Add a layer of mozzarella cheese.

7. Continue making layers of dough and cheese.

8. Drizzle the remaining garlic butter and mozzarella cheese on top.

9. Place the Bundt pan on the smoker and smoke for 45–50 minutes until cheese is melted and pizza dough balls start to lightly brown.

10. Remove and let it cool for a few minutes. Place a plate over the Bundt pan, hold them together, and flip the Bundt pan upside down. Lift the Bundt pan up, leaving the monkey bread on the plate.

11. Top with basil, parsley, and Parmesan while it's still warm. Serve with warm marinara.

Serves 8–10
Prep Time: 15 minutes
Cook Time: 30 minutes
Total Time: 45 minutes

SMOKED QUESO WITH CHORIZO AND POBLANO PEPPERS

This queso is kicked up a notch with the smoky flavor from the Traeger, as well as the addition of chorizo and poblano peppers. Grab a bag of chips and dig in!

9 ounces loose chorizo (out of the casing)
1 poblano pepper
1 block (10 ounces) Oaxaca cheese
1 block (8 ounces) pepper jack cheese

1 block (8 ounces) plain cream cheese
1 cup half-and-half
1 tablespoon chopped fresh cilantro, for garnish
Tortilla chips, for serving

1. Preheat smoker to 350 degrees.

2. Heat a large cast-iron skillet to medium-high heat and cook chorizo, breaking it up with a wooden spoon until slightly darkened and crumbly. Remove chorizo to a bowl and wipe out the remaining grease.

3. Roast the poblano over an open flame on a gas stove or roast in the oven on broil until charred on all sides, about 10 minutes.

4. When poblano has been charred, place it into a bowl and cover with plastic wrap to allow it to steam for about 10 minutes. Then, using a paper towel, remove the charred skin, cut off the stem, and remove the seeds. Dice the pepper and set aside.

5. While the poblano steams, shred the Oaxaca and pepper jack cheeses. Cut the cream cheese into 1-inch cubes.

6. Place the shredded cheeses in the cast-iron skillet and scatter cream cheese cubes throughout. Stir in all but 1 tablespoon diced poblano peppers.

7. Place the skillet in the smoker and smoke for 15 minutes. After 15 minutes, stir completely and smoke another 15 minutes until all the cheeses are combined and melted through.

8. Remove the skillet from the smoker and slowly whisk in half-and-half. Stir to completely combine.

9. Garnish with chorizo, remaining diced poblano peppers, and cilantro. Serve with chips.

PRO TIPS:

- For best results, buy blocks of cheese and grate them yourself or in a food processor.
- You can also substitute the chorizo with seasoned ground beef in this recipe.
- Monterrey Jack or mozzarella cheeses can be substituted for the pepper jack if you don't want the extra spice.

ROASTED TOMATO, FETA & SHRIMP CROSTINI

Serves 6
Prep Time: 5 minutes
Cook Time: 35 minutes
Total Time: 40 minutes

I make this appetizer for a lot of my private chef dinners. It's quick and easy, the flavors come together like magic, and it's always a huge hit!

1 baguette, cut into 1/2-inch slices on a bias
2–3 tablespoons extra virgin olive oil, divided
1 teaspoon kosher salt, divided
1/2 teaspoon black pepper, divided
24 ounces Homemade Marinara (see page 149)

1 block (6 ounces) feta cheese
1/2 pound shrimp (large or 31/35 work best), cleaned and deveined
1/2 tablespoon chopped fresh oregano, for garnish

1. Preheat oven to 400 degrees.

2. Preheat smoker to 425 degrees.

3. Place baguette slices in a single layer on a baking sheet. Drizzle with 1–2 tablespoons olive oil, 1/2 teaspoon salt, and 1/4 teaspoon pepper. Bake on the middle rack of the oven for 10 minutes, until just golden.

4. Add the marinara to a cast-iron skillet. Break the feta into large pieces and drop into the marinara; do not stir.

5. Add the skillet to the smoker and smoke the marinara and feta for 20 minutes.

6. Meanwhile, prepare the shrimp. Dry them completely and drizzle with 1 tablespoon olive oil, 1/2 teaspoon salt, and 1/4 teaspoon pepper.

7. After 20 minutes of smoking, place the shrimp into the sauce. Smoke for another 10–12 minutes until shrimp are opaque and just cooked through.

8. Top with oregano and more feta, if desired, and serve with crostini.

PRO TIPS:

- You can use any size shrimp, but cooking time will need to be adjusted up or down based on size.
- A medium-large shrimp fits well on the crostini.

TANDOORI SMOKED CHICKEN WINGS WITH YOGURT DIPPING SAUCE

Step away from the typical buffalo chicken wings and try these Tandoori Smoked Chicken Wings! They have amazing Middle Eastern flavors with a bright and refreshing yogurt dip.

3 pounds chicken wings, drums, and flats

MARINADE

1 teaspoon kosher salt
1/2 teaspoon black pepper
1 tablespoon garlic powder
1 tablespoon onion powder
1 teaspoon paprika
1 teaspoon harissa

1/2 teaspoon cayenne
1/3 cup plain, whole milk Greek yogurt
1 teaspoon garam masala
1/2 lemon, juiced
3 tablespoons extra virgin olive oil

GREEK YOGURT DIPPING SAUCE

1 cup plain, whole milk Greek yogurt
1 small Persian cucumber, grated and squeezed in
 a paper towel to remove excess water
1 clove of garlic, minced

1/2 lemon, juiced
1 teaspoon kosher salt
1/2 teaspoon black pepper

Squeeze of lemon, for serving
1 tablespoon chopped fresh cilantro, for serving

Kosher salt, for serving

1. Combine the marinade ingredients in a bowl.

2. In a large dish, pour the marinade over the chicken to cover completely. Marinate in the refrigerator for at least 30 minutes or for up to 2 hours. Remove to room temperature 30 minutes prior to grilling.

3. While chicken is marinating, combine the dipping sauce ingredients in a bowl. Set aside.

4. Preheat the smoker to 375 degrees. Remove chicken from marinade, allowing the excess to drip off, and place on a parchment-lined baking sheet with a rack.

5. Smoke chicken for 20 minutes.

6. Increase temperature to 425 degrees and smoke for 15 minutes.

7. Flip and smoke for 10 more minutes.

8. Serve chicken on a platter with the yogurt dipping sauce, a squeeze of lemon, cilantro, and a sprinkle of salt.

GARLIC LEMON PEPPER WINGS

Serves 6–8
Prep Time: 40 minutes
Cook Time: 40 minutes
Total Time: 1 hour, 20 minutes

Our teenage boys have a slight chicken wing obsession, and that's putting it mildly . . . they eat them at least once a week! Lemon pepper is one of their favorite flavors, so this is a recipe I created to make them at home.

4 pounds chicken wings
Lemon wedges, for garnish (optional)

Parsley, for garnish (optional)

LEMON PEPPER DRY RUB

1 tablespoon lemon pepper seasoning
1 tablespoon kosher salt
1 tablespoon garlic powder

1 tablespoon onion powder
2 tablespoons cornstarch

GARLIC LEMON PEPPER SAUCE

8 tablespoons salted butter
3 cloves of garlic, minced
1 lemon, zested and juiced

1 teaspoon kosher salt
1/4 teaspoon black pepper

1. Pat wings completely dry with paper towels. Spread them out on a rack-lined baking sheet and place in the refrigerator uncovered for at least 30 minutes.

2. Combine the lemon pepper dry rub ingredients in a small bowl.

3. Preheat the smoker to 400 degrees.

4. Remove the wings from the refrigerator and place them in a large baking dish. Coat them with the rub on all sides and then with the cornstarch, mixing it until the cornstarch is incorporated into the rub on the wings and is no longer powder white.

5. Smoke the wings for 20 minutes. Turn and smoke another 15–20 minutes until cooked through and crisp.

6. Meanwhile, in a saucepan, combine the garlic lemon pepper sauce ingredients. Bring to a simmer for the butter to melt and keep warm on lowest setting.

7. Toss the wings with the sauce in a large bowl. Plate on a large serving platter with lemon wedges and parsley.

"STADIUM STYLE" SMOKED CHICKEN NACHOS

Are you team "shredded cheese" or team "stadium style"? While shredded cheese nachos are delicious in their own right, I wanted to create a "stadium style" nacho with melty cheese to munch on during game day to remind you of being at the game in person.

6 boneless, skinless chicken thighs (about 2 pounds)

3 tablespoons of your favorite seasoning (I like Meat Church Fajita seasoning)

1 tablespoon extra virgin olive oil

1 cup chicken stock

1 bag of your favorite tortilla chips

1 can (15 ounces) black beans, drained and rinsed

1 jalapeño, diced

4 scallions, sliced

6 ounces pico de gallo

2 tablespoons chopped fresh cilantro

4 ounces guacamole

4 ounces sour cream

QUESO

1 block (8 ounces) cheddar cheese, shredded

1 block (8 ounces) Monterey Jack cheese, shredded

1/2 cup heavy cream

1. Preheat smoker to 400 degrees.

2. Coat both sides of the chicken with olive oil and your favorite seasoning.

3. Sear chicken on the smoker, about 5 minutes per side, just to wake up the spices.

4. Add chicken to a foil container with chicken stock. Smoke, uncovered, for about 30 minutes until tender.

5. Remove chicken and shred into a bowl, adding cooking juices to the chicken to keep it from getting dry.

6. In a saucepan, add the queso ingredients. Stir constantly over medium-low heat until cheese is completely melted and has a smooth consistency.

7. On a platter, spread chips in a single layer and add some of the chicken, queso, beans, jalapeños, scallions, pico de gallo, and cilantro.

8. Add a few more layers of chips and toppings. On the final layer, add a dollop of guacamole and sour cream.

POULTRY

SMOKED CHICKEN THIGHS & SUMMER SUCCOTASH

Serves 4–6
Prep Time: 15 minutes
Cook Time: 45 minutes
Total Time: 1 hour

Chicken thighs are one of my favorite things to smoke on my Traeger. They always come out with crispy skin and so juicy! This is a great light and easy dish to enjoy all summer long.

8 chicken thighs

3 tablespoons extra virgin olive oil

CHICKEN RUB

1 tablespoon kosher salt

1 teaspoon black pepper

1 tablespoon ground cumin

1 tablespoon ground coriander

SUMMER SUCCOTASH

1 shallot, sliced

2 cloves of garlic, minced

2 ears of corn, kernels cut from the cob

1/2 red bell pepper, thinly sliced

1 zucchini, sliced on a 1-inch bias

1 summer squash, sliced on a 1-inch bias

1 tablespoon fresh basil, for garnish

1 tablespoon fresh cilantro, for garnish

1 teaspoon smoked paprika

1 teaspoon garlic powder

1 teaspoon onion powder

1/8 teaspoon cayenne (optional)

12 cherry tomatoes

1 tablespoon extra virgin olive oil

1 teaspoon kosher salt

1/2 teaspoon black pepper

1 tablespoon red wine vinegar

1. Preheat smoker to 375 degrees.

2. While the smoker heats, trim excess fat from the chicken thighs and place in a bowl. Drizzle with olive oil.

3. Combine the chicken rub ingredients in a small bowl.

4. Sprinkle the rub over the chicken, coating all sides.

5. Place chicken skin-side down on the smoker and smoke for 20 minutes.

6. While the chicken is cooking, prepare the vegetables. Add the shallot, garlic, corn, bell pepper, zucchini, squash, and tomatoes to a large skillet. Toss with olive oil, salt, and pepper.

7. After 20 minutes of smoking, increase the smoker's temperature to 400 degrees and flip the chicken. Add the skillet of vegetables to the smoker and close the lid. Cook for an additional 20–25 minutes, stirring the vegetables midway through. The internal temperature of the chicken should register at 165 degrees when it is done.

8. Remove the chicken and vegetables from the smoker and toss the vegetables with red wine vinegar. Serve on a platter with the chicken; garnish with basil and cilantro.

Serves 6–8
Prep Time: 20 minutes
Cook Time: 2 hours, 30 minutes
Total Time: 2 hours, 50 minutes

SMOKED CHICKEN ENCHILADAS

Smoked chicken enchiladas are the perfect weeknight dinner! If you want to cut down on the prep time, pick up a cooked rotisserie chicken to shred and pick up a few large jars of your favorite salsa verde.

1 fryer rotisserie chicken
3 tablespoons All-Purpose Seasoning (see page 134), or your favorite dry rub
Salsa Verde, divided (see page 140)
2–3 cups shredded Monterey Jack cheese, divided

12 tortillas, corn or flour
Sour cream, for garnish
Crumbled cotija cheese, for garnish
Fresh cilantro, for garnish
Lime wedges, for garnish

1. Preheat smoker to 375 degrees.

2. Spatchcock the chicken by removing the backbone with kitchen shears and pressing on the breastbone to make it flat. Tuck the wings behind the chicken. Pat completely dry and season with All-Purpose Seasoning or your favorite rub.

3. Smoke for about 1 hour, 15 minutes, depending upon the size or until it registers 165 degrees with an instant-read thermomete.

4. When the chicken is finished, remove it, allow to cool, and shred the meat into a bowl, removing the skin and bones.

5. To the bowl of shredded chicken, add 1 cup Salsa Verde and 1 cup Monterey Jack cheese. Stir to combine.

6. Add 1/2 cup Salsa Verde to the bottom of a cast-iron baking dish.

7. Pour some of the Salsa Verde into a shallow bowl and dip a tortilla into the Salsa Verde, coating both sides. Place a scoop of the chicken mixture into the tortilla and roll it. Place it seam-side down into the pan. Continue this process until all enchiladas are rolled. Place them snugly together in the pan. Top with the remaining Salsa Verde and 1–2 cups Monterrey Jack cheese. Cover the pan with aluminum foil.

8. Place the enchiladas on the smoker and cook for 30 minutes covered.

9. Remove the foil and increase the smoker's temperature to 400 degrees. Cook for an additional 20–30 minutes until cheese is melted and bubbly.

10. Garnish with sour cream, crumbled cotija cheese, cilantro, and lime wedges.

SMOKED CHICKEN POT PIE

Serves 4
Prep Time: 15 minutes
Cook Time: 1 hour, 10 minutes
Total Time: 1 hour, 25 minutes

This recipe is so easy and so delicious on the smoker—it's comfort food the whole family will love!

3–5 tablespoons extra virgin olive oil, divided

2 tablespoons of your favorite rub

3 bone-in, skin-on chicken breasts

3 carrots, sliced into 1/4-inch slices

2 celery stalks, sliced into 1/4-inch slices

1 leek, sliced into 1/4-inch slices, white and light green parts only

3 cloves of garlic, minced

1 teaspoon kosher salt, plus more to taste

1/2 teaspoon black pepper, plus more to taste

1 teaspoon chopped fresh thyme, plus more for garnish

1 tablespoon chopped fresh parsley

2 tablespoons all-purpose flour

2 tablespoons sherry wine

1 1/2 cups chicken stock

1 cup heavy cream

1/2 cup frozen green peas

1 package puff pastry dough, such as Dufour

Egg wash (1 egg beaten with 1 tablespoon water)

1. Preheat smoker to 400 degrees.

2. Add 2–3 tablespoons olive oil and your favorite rub to chicken breasts. Place on a small baking sheet and put on the center rack of smoker. Cook for 20–25 minutes, until the internal temperature registers 165 degrees. Once cooked, remove and allow to cool.

3. Increase smoker to 425 degrees. Meanwhile, heat a large skillet (recommended 12 inches) over medium-low heat. Add 1–2 tablespoons olive oil, carrots, celery, and leeks. Sauté over medium-low heat until translucent, about 8 minutes.

4. Add garlic, salt, pepper, thyme, and parsley. Stir to combine and sauté for 1 more minute.

5. Sprinkle flour over the vegetable mixture and stir to combine. Cook for 2 minutes until coated. Add sherry and cook for 2 minutes until evaporated.

6. Increase heat to medium, add chicken stock, and bring to a simmer. Using a wooden spoon, scrape up any browned bits from the bottom of the pan. Add the heavy cream and stir. Simmer for 2–3 minutes and then remove from heat to allow the pan to cool.

7. When the chicken has cooled, remove and discard the skin; then shred the chicken.

8. Add the chicken, along with any juices that accumulated in the pan, to the vegetable mixture. Add peas and stir to combine. Taste the mixture to check for seasoning; add salt and pepper if needed.

9. Trim the puff pastry dough in a circle shape and roll out so it covers the skillet. Place the dough on top of the vegetable mixture and press the edges to form a seal. Using a paring knife, cut a few small slits in the crust to allow the steam to escape. Brush with egg wash and sprinkle with salt.

10. Place chicken pot pie in the center of the smoker and smoke for 25–30 minutes, until golden brown.

11. Sprinkle fresh thyme and more salt, if desired, on top and serve.

PRO TIPS:

- Save the chicken bones and the vegetable scraps to make chicken stock.

- You can use a cooked rotisserie chicken to save time.

Serves 6
Prep Time: 15 minutes
Cook Time: 10 minutes
Total Time: 25 minutes

CHICKEN CAPRESE SANDWICHES

This sandwich is a creation of ALL my favorite things! If I could design the perfect sandwich that I'd want to see on a restaurant menu, this would be it!

3 chicken breasts
1 large tomato, sliced into 1/4-inch slices
1 block (8 ounces) fresh mozzarella, thinly sliced
Kosher salt to taste
Black pepper to taste

Basil Pesto (see page 136)
6 slices thick-cut bacon
6 ciabatta buns
2–3 tablespoons extra virgin olive oil
1–2 tablespoons balsamic vinegar

1. Slice chicken breasts through the center lengthwise.

2. Sprinkle tomato and mozzarella slices with salt and pepper.

3. Use 1/4 cup Basil Pesto to coat all sides of the chicken; reserve the rest for the sandwiches.

4. Preheat oven to 400 degrees and cook bacon, flipping once, until crisp. Remove to a paper towel–lined plate to drain. Break in half and set aside for the sandwiches.

5. Preheat grill to medium heat and spray with non-stick spray.

6. Sear the chicken about 4–5 minutes. They will be ready to flip when they release from the grill without tearing.

7. After you flip the chicken, reduce the heat to medium-low and add two slices of mozzarella and tomato to each chicken breast. Tent with a large sheet of foil or cover with dome lids to help melt the cheese. Grill another 5 minutes until chicken is cooked through.

8. Meanwhile, drizzle each bun with olive oil and place on the side of the grill to toast with indirect heat.

9. To build, spread reserved pesto on the inside of each toasted bun, add a chicken breast with mozzarella and tomato, drizzle with balsamic vinegar, top with bacon, and add the top bun.

Serves 6
Prep Time: 15 minutes
Marinade Time: 1 hour
Cook Time: 20 minutes
Total Time: 1 hour, 35 minutes

HULI HULI CHICKEN SKEWERS

In Hawaiian, *huli huli* means "turn, turn." This is a recipe you want to turn or rotate every few minutes for even cooking and delicious results . . . they are *ono* ("delicious")!

MARINADE

1/3 cup brown sugar

1/3 cup soy sauce

1/3 cup ketchup

2 tablespoons honey or agave

1/4 cup sherry wine

3 tablespoons sesame oil

1 teaspoon Worcestershire sauce

1 tablespoon chipotle peppers in adobo sauce

3 tablespoons rice vinegar

1/4 cup chicken stock

3 cloves of garlic, grated

1 tablespoon grated fresh ginger

4 boneless, skinless chicken breasts, cut into 1–2-inch chunks

1 1/2 teaspoons kosher salt, divided, plus more to taste

1/2 teaspoon black pepper, plus more to taste

1/2 pineapple, core removed and cut into 1–2-inch chunks

1 red bell pepper, seeds removed and cut into 1–2-inch chunks

1 yellow onion, cut into 1–2-inch chunks

2 tablespoons vegetable oil

2 scallions, dark green parts only, sliced on a bias, for garnish

1. Combine the marinade ingredients in a bowl.

2. Add the chicken in a single layer to a large dish with deep sides; sprinkle with 1 teaspoon salt and 1/2 teaspoon pepper.

3. Divide the marinade into thirds: 1/3 will be for marinating, 1/3 will be for basting, and 1/3 will be for serving.

4. Pour 1/3 of the marinade over the chicken and marinate for about 1 hour, but no longer than 2 hours, flipping halfway through to coat all sides. Remove from the refrigerator 30 minutes before grilling to bring to room temperature.

5. In a large bowl, combine the pineapple, bell pepper, and onion with vegetable oil and 1/2 teaspoon salt; stir to coat.

6. Preheat the grill to medium and spray grill grates with non-stick spray.

7. On a skewer, alternate adding chicken, pineapple, bell pepper, and onion until each skewer is full. When adding the pieces to the skewer, don't pack them too tightly to ensure heat has room to flow for even cooking. Lightly season each side of each skewer with additional salt and pepper.

8. Rotate the skewers about every 4 minutes, until all sides have nice color and are cooked through. As you turn them, baste each side with 1/3 of the marinade. It will probably take about 20 minutes total cooking time.

9. Garnish with scallions and serve with the remaining 1/3 of the marinade for dipping.

PRO TIPS:

- You can use boneless, skinless chicken thighs if you prefer, but cooking time may vary. Always make sure chicken is cooked to an internal temperature of 165 degrees.

- If you are using wooden skewers, be sure to soak them in water at least 1 hour prior to grilling so they don't burn.

- Another variation of this recipe is to grill just the chicken and pineapple if you want to leave out the peppers and onions.

ARROZ CON POLLO

I love one-pan meals! Especially when I'm cooking outside and can throw it all together and jump in the pool while it cooks. I love the addition of Chimichurri and pickled red onions to this recipe—they add a punch of great flavors!

RUB

1 tablespoon cumin

1 tablespoon coriander

1/2 tablespoon oregano

1 tablespoon kosher salt

1 teaspoon black pepper

1 tablespoon pimentón or sub smoked paprika

1/4 teaspoon cayenne

1/2 tablespoon garlic powder

1/2 tablespoon onion powder

6 bone-in, skin-on chicken thighs

2–3 tablespoons extra virgin olive oil

1 yellow onion, diced

5 cloves of garlic, minced

2 bay leaves

1 can (28 ounces) diced tomatoes and their juices

2 cups long grain rice

3 cups chicken stock, adding more if needed

1 teaspoon kosher salt

1/2 teaspoon black pepper

1/8 teaspoon saffron threads

1/4 cup peas

Chimichurri, for garnish (see page 139)

Pickled Red Onions, for garnish (see page 142)

1. Preheat smoker to 400 degrees.

2. Combine the rub ingredients in a bowl.

3. Coat chicken with the rub and set aside for 30 minutes at room temperature.

4. In a large sauté pan with deep sides, heat to medium heat for 60–90 seconds. Then add olive oil, swirl to coat, and heat 30 seconds. Add the chicken, skin-side down, and sear for 4 minutes; flip and sear the other side for 4 minutes. Remove to a plate.

5. Lower the heat to medium-low. In the same sauté pan, heat onion for 5 minutes until softened but not browned. Add garlic and cook for another minute. Add bay leaves, tomatoes, rice, chicken stock, salt, pepper, and saffron.

6. Bring to a boil before reducing to a simmer, scraping the browned bits from the bottom of the pan with a wooden spoon. Add the chicken back in, skin-side up. Turn the heat off and transfer the pan to the smoker.

7. Smoke for 30 minutes until chicken is cooked through and rice is tender and has absorbed most of the liquid. During the last 5 minutes of cooking, add peas.

8. When the chicken is finished, plate with rice, Chimichurri, and Pickled Red Onions.

SMOKED BBQ CHICKEN WITH GOCHUJANG BBQ SAUCE

Serves 4–6
Prep Time: 5 minutes
Marinade Time: 30 minutes
Cook Time: 40 minutes
Total Time: 1 hour, 15 minutes

I was so excited to create this recipe! I absolutely love BBQ chicken; we enjoy it all year round. I had the idea to take it to the next level by incorporating the umami-driven, sweet-heat flavors of gochujang into my homemade BBQ sauce, and I couldn't be happier with the result! This is now our family's favorite BBQ chicken recipe!

4 pounds chicken—drumsticks, thighs, breasts
4–5 tablespoons All-Purpose Seasoning (see page 134), or your favorite seasoning
Gochujang BBQ Sauce, divided (see page 146)

2 scallions, green parts only, sliced on a long bias for garnish
Toasted sesame seeds for garnish

1. Pat chicken dry with paper towels; trim excess fat if necessary.

2. Coat all sides of the chicken with seasoning. Let chicken sit at room temperature for 30 minutes to allow the rub to adhere to the chicken.

3. Preheat the smoker to 400 degrees.

4. Place the chicken, skin-side down, on the smoker and close the lid. Smoke undisturbed for 15 minutes.

5. Flip chicken and smoke another 15–20 minutes or until the chicken reaches an internal temperature of 165 degrees.

6. Use a basting brush to coat all sides of the chicken with 1 cup Gochujang BBQ Sauce and smoke, skin-side up, for 5 more minutes.

7. Serve with remaining Gochujang BBQ Sauce.

PRO TIP:

- Cooking times may vary, depending on the size of the chicken pieces you are using. It's always best to use a probe to notify you when it is cooked to at least 165 degrees. For this recipe, total cooking time is 35–40 minutes; however, chicken breasts may cook faster, so adjust the cooking time down by 5 minutes if necessary.

Serves 4–6
Prep Time: 15 minutes
Marinade Time: 30 minutes
Cook Time: 15 minutes
Total Time: 1 hour

GREEK-INSPIRED CHICKEN SOUVLAKI SKEWERS

This recipe is inspired by my Greek mother-in-law; she has cooked us some amazing Greek food over the years! Chicken souvlaki skewers have always been one of my favorites, so I took the dish and added a few of my own touches. Served with tzatziki sauce, warm naan, and Greek salad, when all the flavors fill the plate is my absolute favorite!

4 boneless, skinless chicken breasts, cut into
   1-inch chunks
2 teaspoons kosher salt, divided
1 teaspoon black pepper, divided

MARINADE
2 lemons, zested and juiced
3 cloves of garlic, minced
1 teaspoon dill
1/2 tablespoon oregano

Tzatziki Sauce, for serving (see page 137)
Warm naan, for serving
Greek Salad, for serving (see page 112)

1/3 cup extra virgin olive oil
1 teaspoon salt
1/2 teaspoon pepper

1.	Place the chicken in a large bowl. In a small bowl, whisk together the marinade ingredients. Add to the bowl of chicken and turn to coat. Marinate between 30 minutes and 2 hours. Refrigerate if not grilling within an hour.

2.	Preheat the grill to medium-low.

3.	Skewer the chunks of chicken and sprinkle all sides with 1 teaspoon salt and 1/2 teaspoon pepper.

4.	Spray the grill with non-stick spray. Add the chicken skewers to the grill and close the lid. Cook for 4–5 minutes to allow for grill marks.

5.	Turn each skewer 90 degrees and cook another 4 minutes. Continue cooking at 90-degree turns until all sides are grilled and chicken is cooked through, about 15 minutes.

6.	Remove from the grill and serve with Tzatziki Sauce, warm naan, and Greek Salad.

PRO TIPS:

•	If using wooden skewers, be sure to soak them in water for at least an hour to avoid burning them on the grill.

•	When skewering the chicken, do not pack them super tight—allow a little space between each piece.

CHICKEN STREET TACOS

Serves 4–6
Prep Time: 10 minutes
Cook Time: 10 minutes
Total Time: 20 minutes

Taco Tuesday on your table in less than 30 minutes! Street tacos are simple ingredients done right to make a great bite!

4 chicken breasts
2 tablespoons Meat Church Fajita seasoning, or your favorite seasoning
1 Tablespoon chipotle in adobo sauce
1 tablespoon extra virgin olive oil
2–3 tablespoons vegetable oil

1 lime, halved horizontally
Corn or flour tortillas, warmed
1/2 yellow onion, diced, for serving
2 tablespoons roughly chopped fresh cilantro, for serving

1. Preheat the griddle to medium-high heat.

2. Slice the chicken breasts through the center horizontally and sprinkle with seasoning. Add to a bowl with adobo sauce and olive oil; stir to coat the chicken.

3. Add vegetable oil to the griddle, allow to heat, and add the chicken to the griddle. Cook 3–4 minutes per side or until cooked through. Remove to a plate.

4. Juice half of the lime and slice the remaining half into wedges for serving.

5. Dice the chicken breasts into bite-sized chunks and combine with lime juice.

6. Serve in warm tortillas with lime wedges, onion, and cilantro.

CHICKEN PESTO PIZZA

We have a pizza oven at our house and are always making new creations. Every time our kids have friends over or we invite one of their sports teams over for a team party, we end up throwing some pizzas into the mix. This combo has always been a family favorite.

2 cups shredded mozzarella cheese, divided
1 chicken breast, roasted and thinly sliced
1 Roma tomato, thinly sliced lengthwise
5 mushrooms, thinly sliced
1/3 small red onion, thinly sliced
1–2 tablespoons extra virgin olive oil

1 can (13.8 ounces) pizza dough
1 cup Basil Pesto, divided (see page 136)
1 teaspoon dried Italian seasoning
Fresh basil, torn, for garnish
Grated Parmesan cheese, for garnish

1. Preheat the smoker to 450 degrees.

2. In a large bowl, mix together 1 cup mozzarella, chicken, tomatoes, mushrooms, and onions.

3. Evenly coat the bottom and sides of a cast-iron pan with olive oil.

4. Roll pizza dough into a large round shape and place it into the pan, pressing the dough about halfway up the sides.

5. Spread a layer of pesto onto the flat section of dough; then top with the chicken-mozzarella mixture.

6. Sprinkle Italian seasoning and the remaining mozzarella on top.

7. Place the cast-iron pan in the smoker and smoke the pizza for 30–35 minutes until edges are golden brown. Remove and drizzle the remaining pesto over the top.

8. Top with basil and Parmesan cheese, if desired. Slice and serve!

PRO TIPS:

- You can also use rotisserie chicken for this recipe.
- Store-bought pesto is also an option, instead of homemade.

Serves 4–6
Prep Time: 30 minutes
Marinade Time: 10 minutes
Cook Time: 1 hour, 30 minutes
Total Time: 2 hours, 10 minutes

CHICKEN QUESABIRRIA

Quesabirria tacos are typically made with beef or goat meat. This is my lightened-up version with chicken instead. The Fire-Roasted Salsa is optional because you already have the consommé dipping sauce; however, it makes a great addition to the dish!

5 guajillo dried chiles

3 ancho dried chiles

3 dried chiles de árbol

10 chicken thighs (about 4 pounds)

2 tablespoons extra virgin olive oil

1 1/2 yellow onions, diced, divided

1 tablespoon kosher salt, plus more to taste

5 cloves of garlic, sliced

1 can (28 ounces) San Marzano tomatoes, whole

1/4 cup apple cider vinegar

2 cups chicken stock

1 chipotle pepper in adobo sauce (add one more for additional spice)

2 bay leaves

1 cinnamon stick

2 tablespoons vegetable oil

10–12 taco-size tortillas

1 block (10 ounces) Oaxaca cheese, shredded

1/4 cup chopped fresh cilantro, for garnish

Fire-Roasted Salsa (see page 133)

RUB

1/2 teaspoon ground cloves

1 tablespoon cumin

1 tablespoon coriander

1 tablespoon oregano

1 tablespoon kosher salt

1 teaspoon black pepper

1. In a large cast-iron pot, add the dried peppers and cover them with boiling water. Steep for 20 minutes until softened.

2. Combine the rub ingredients in a shallow bowl and then apply the rub to all sides of the chicken. Allow to sit at room temperature while you preheat smoker to 425 degrees.

3. Transfer chiles to a cutting board, remove stems and seeds, and place in a blender. Strain 1 cup of the rehydrating chili liquid and add it to the blender. Discard the remaining liquid.

4. In the same cast-iron pot, add olive oil and heat to medium-low. Add 1 diced onion and salt; sauté for about 7 minutes until translucent. Add garlic and sauté 2 minutes. Add tomatoes and bring to a boil before reducing to a simmer. Allow to simmer about 15 minutes to meld the flavors. Turn off the heat and allow to cool.

5. Add the onion, garlic, and tomato mixture; apple cider vinegar; chicken stock; and chipotle pepper to the peppers in the blender. Blend and then add this consommé braising liquid back to the pot. Add the bay leaves and cinnamon stick; then place the pot on the smoker.

6. Add the chicken thighs to the smoker and sear the chicken, about 5 minutes per side to bring out the spice rub flavors. Chicken will not be cooked through, but it will continue to cook as it braises.

7. Add seared chicken to the pot of consommé braising liquid. Reduce heat to 350 degrees. Braise for 60–90 minutes (the longer, the more smoke flavor will be achieved).

8. Remove the pot of chicken from the smoker; discard the bay leaves and cinnamon stick. Taste and add more salt if needed.

9. Add the chicken to a separate bowl. Remove and discard the bones and skin; then shred the chicken and add a few ladles of the braising liquid to keep it moist.

10. Preheat the griddle to medium heat. Add vegetable oil to the griddle.

11. Dip the tortillas in the top layer of the remaining braising liquid, dipping them only so far as the accumulated top layer of fat so they will crisp up, and add them to the griddle. Add shredded chicken to half of each tortilla, along with some Oaxaca cheese. Fold in half and then flip until both sides are crispy.

12. Remove and top with cilantro and onions. Pour the reserved consommé into serving bowls or dip in the Fire-Roasted Salsa.

PRO TIPS:

- It is important to shallowly dip the tortillas into the top layer of the consommé; you are trying to coat them with the layer of cooking fat, instead of the sauce, so they don't stick to the griddle.

PORK

Serves 4
Prep Time: 15 minutes
Marinade Time: 30 minutes
Cook Time: 1 hour, 10 minutes
Total Time: 1 hour, 55 minutes

DOUBLE-CUT PORK CHOPS WITH BOURBON PEACH JALAPEÑO GLAZE

Double-cut pork chops are one of my husband's favorite summer meals! For Father's Day, I wanted to create a glaze that he would love, and this sweet and spicy combo definitely hit the spot!

2 double-cut, bone-in pork chops

RUB
1/2 tablespoon kosher salt

1 teaspoon black pepper

1 teaspoon garlic powder

1 teaspoon smoked paprika

BOURBON PEACH JALAPEÑO GLAZE
4 tablespoons butter

1 cup peach preserves

1/2 cup bourbon of choice

2 tablespoons apple cider vinegar

1/2 teaspoon kosher salt

1/2 teaspoon black pepper

1/2 jalapeño, sliced lengthwise, seeds and ribs removed

1. Preheat smoker to 275 degrees.

2. Combine the rub ingredients in a small bowl and then season pork chops on all sides with rub. Let them sit at room temperature for 30 minutes.

3. Smoke pork chops until they reach about 125 degrees; use a heat-safe thermometer probe, if possible, for accuracy.

4. Remove pork chops to a plate and increase smoker temperature to 425 degrees. Set a cast-iron pan inside to heat.

5. Combine the bourbon peach jalapeño glaze ingredients in a small pot on the stovetop. Stir to combine and simmer for about 15 minutes while smoker is heating. Reserve half of the glaze in a separate bowl to use as a dipping sauce.

6. Brush the glaze over all sides of the pork chops and add them to the smoker in the cast-iron pan. Sear for 5 minutes, flip, and sear the other side for 5 minutes. If there is a fat cap around the edges, sear the sides for 1–2 minutes on all sides to render. They are finished when the internal temperature is 140 degrees.

7. Remove them to a cutting board and tent with foil to rest for 10 minutes.

8. Brush the pork chops with another coat of the reserved marinade; slice, and serve with the remaining marinade as a dipping sauce.

PRO TIP:

*   Serve with grilled peaches as the perfect accompaniment! Brush them with a neutral oil and grill for a few minutes, flesh-side down, to get some grill marks.

SWEET & SPICY PORK TENDERLOIN BOWLS

Serves 4–6
Prep Time: 15 minutes
Marinade Time: 30 minutes
Cook Time: 15 minutes
Total Time: 1 hour

A fun and creative recipe in a bowl, combining the sweet and spicy flavors in the pork with delicious crisp veggies . . . because doesn't everything taste better in a bowl?

MARINADE

3 tablespoons gochujang

3 tablespoons soy sauce

2 tablespoons honey

2 tablespoons rice vinegar

1 tablespoon minced garlic

1 tablespoon minced ginger

1 tablespoon sesame oil

2 pork tenderloins (about 1 1/2 pounds each), sliced into thin strips 1/4" thick

3 heads baby bok choy

2 cups shitake mushrooms

2 cups snap peas

4 tablespoons vegetable oil, divided

1/2 teaspoon kosher salt

1/4 teaspoon black pepper

1 tablespoon chopped fresh cilantro, for garnish

1 tablespoon julienned Thai basil, for garnish

1 red fresno chile, thinly sliced for garnish (optional)

Coconut Cilantro Rice, for serving (see page 127)

1. Combine the marinade ingredients in a small bowl, whisk to combine, and add to a large ziplock bag.

2. Add the pork to the ziplock and marinate at room temperature for 30–60 minutes.

3. Clean the bok choy and slice the leaves in half vertically, top to bottom. Clean the mushrooms, removing the dirt with a damp paper towel; then remove the stems and slice into strips lengthwise. Clean and trim the stems of the snap peas.

4. Preheat the griddle over medium-high heat. Add the vegetable oil, spreading across the surface to coat the cooking area. Remove the pork from the marinade, allowing excess to drip off. Add it to the griddle in a single layer and cook undisturbed for about 4 minutes.

5. Use a large spatula to flip the pork to the other side and cook another 4–5 minutes until sear and color are achieved on all sides. Remove to a bowl.

6. Add vegetable oil to the griddle; then add bok choy, mushrooms, snap peas, salt, and pepper. Sauté for about 5 minutes until the vegetables are cooked.

7. Serve in a bowl with sautéed vegetables and Coconut Cilantro Rice.

8. Garnish with chopped cilantro and Thai basil. Add red fresno chiles if desired.

Serves 4–6
Prep Time: 10 minutes
Marinade Time: 30 minutes
Cook Time: 3 hours, 30 minutes
Total Time: 4 hours, 10 minutes

"FOIL BOAT" SMOKED ST. LOUIS RIBS

Around here, BBQ ribs are smoked all year long—everyone loves them! This has come to be my favorite method and timing for tender ribs, where you can still take a bite without them completely falling off the bone.

2 racks St. Louis–style ribs
4 tablespoons yellow mustard
2 tablespoons Meat Church Texas Sugar BBQ Rub, or dry rub of your choice
2 tablespoons Meat Church Holy Gospel BBQ Rub, or dry rub of your choice

Spritzes of equal parts apple juice and apple cider vinegar
8 tablespoons butter, divided
6 tablespoons brown sugar, divided
BBQ sauce of your choice

1. Preheat smoker to 250 degrees.

2. Remove membrane from the back side of the ribs. Coat meat side of ribs with mustard and cover all sides with Meat Church Texas Sugar BBQ Rub and Meat Church Holy Gospel BBQ Rub. Let sit at room temperature for 30 minutes.

3. Smoke, meat-side up, for 2 hours. After 1 hour, spritz with apple juice and apple cider vinegar. Spritz again after 1 1/2 hours.

4. Tear 2 large pieces of heavy-duty foil for each rack of ribs and add 4 tablespoons butter and evenly sprinkle 3 tablespoons brown sugar in the center of each piece of foil.

5. Place the ribs, meat-side down, onto the butter and brown sugar and spritz with apple juice and apple cider vinegar again. Fold and wrap the edges of the foil tightly against all sides of the rack of ribs to hold in the juices, leaving the top bone–side exposed.

6. Increase smoker temperature to 275 degrees and return to the smoker. Smoke for another 60–90 minutes.

7. Remove, flip the racks of ribs over in the foil boat to expose the meat side, brush with your favorite BBQ sauce, and return to the smoker one last time, meat-side up, for 30 minutes until sauce is set.

PRO TIPS:

- This recipe and method can also be used for baby back ribs.

- If you want more of a fall-off-the-bone rib, increase smoke time in step 6 to 2 hours.

SMOKED PORK CHILE VERDE

Serves 6
Prep Time: 5 minutes
Cook Time: 25 minutes
Total Time: 30 minutes

Just thinking about this recipe makes my mouth water! Braising the pork in the spices and fresh flavors of the chile verde until it is fall-apart tender is the ultimate!

4 pounds boneless pork shoulder
Mexican Spice Rub (see page 135)
2 tablespoons extra virgin olive oil
Salsa Verde (see page 140)
2 cups chicken stock

Tortillas or rice, for serving
Chopped fresh cilantro, for serving
Crumbled cotija cheese, for serving
Lime wedges, for serving

1. Preheat the smoker to 350 degrees.

2. Trim most of the fat from the pork shoulder and cut into 2-inch cubes. Coat all sides generously with the Mexican Spice Rub.

3. Heat a large cast-iron Dutch oven over medium-high heat and add olive oil. Add half of the pork shoulder chunks to the pan, searing each side for about 3 minutes. Remove to a separate bowl and repeat searing with remaining meat until all meat has been seared.

4. Add all the meat and any accumulated juices back to the Dutch oven pan. Add the Salsa Verde and chicken stock and stir to combine.

5. Make a paper lid (cartouche) by folding a large piece of parchment paper in half and in half again; then folding the corners in to make a triangle and fold it one final time. Cut a small hole on the folded point. Open the paper lid and use it to cover the entire Dutch oven, pressing completely to the sides so it stays on.

6. Smoke chile verde for 2 hours.

7. Remove cartouche, stir, and smoke 1 additional hour, uncovered, until fork tender.

8. Serve chile verde with tortillas or rice. Optional toppings include cilantro, cotija cheese, and lime wedges.

PRO TIPS:

- When searing the pork, sear over medium-high heat so it doesn't blacken. You want to be able to use the browned bits at the bottom of the pan to enhance the chile verde sauce. If it's getting too dark, turn the heat down to medium.

- For a spicier option, leave seeds and ribs in the jalapeños.

- If you don't have a cast-iron Dutch oven for your smoker, you can use an aluminum tin and cover with a square piece of parchment paper, cutting a hole in the middle for steam to escape and allow pork to braise until tender.

Serves 8–10
Prep Time: 10 minutes
Marinade Time: 24 hours
Cook Time: 12 hours
Total Time: 36 hours, 10 minutes

KALUA PORK

Kalua pork is one of those dishes that is so simple, without too many ingredients, but it is so tender and delicious! Because I'm not building the traditional "imu" (an underground oven) in my yard anytime soon, I came up with this version to get a similar smoky effect. I even wrapped the pork in banana leaves to add that sweet traditional Hawaiian flavor. It's great to make a large portion of it and serve it at a party! In the following recipes, I've showed how to use the leftovers a few different ways, so make a big batch!

6 pounds boneless pork shoulder

2 tablespoons Maldon Smoked Sea Salt

2 tablespoons Ono Hawaiian salt seasoning

2 large banana leaves

1. Pat the pork shoulder dry and score fat cap about 1/4-inch deep, in a cross hatch.

2. Season all sides of the boneless pork shoulder with salts. Wrap tightly in plastic wrap, so no air can get in. Place in a bowl or on a sheet pan in case juices leak and refrigerate overnight for 24 hours.

3. Preheat smoker to 225 degrees and turn on the super smoke (if your smoker has that function).

4. Remove the pork from the plastic wrap and let come to room temperature, about 30 minutes, before smoking.

5. Smoke pork, fat cap up, for 2 hours.

6. Remove pork and turn off super smoke.

7. Wrap the smoked pork shoulder with 2 overlapping layers of banana leaves, tucking them tightly around the pork.

8. Double wrap the pork shoulder and banana leaves in heavy foil. Place entire pork shoulder into an aluminum tin pan to collect the juices.

9. Smoke the pork shoulder for 10 hours.

10. Remove, let cool slightly, and remove foil and banana leaves, unwrapping it in the foil tin to collect all the cooking juices.

11. Remove the fat cap and as much fat as possible and shred the pork with your hands or two forks into the tin pan with the cooking juices to keep it moist.

PRO TIP:

- If you cannot find Ono Hawaiian salt seasoning, kosher salt is a good substitute.

KALUA PORK SANDWICHES WITH CITRUS SLAW & PINEAPPLE CHUTNEY

6 brioche or Hawaiian rolls
Kalua Pork (see page 54)

Citrus Slaw (see page 57)
Pineapple Chutney (see page 58)

1. Assemble the sandwiches with the Kalua Pork on the bottom half.
2. Spread the top half with Pineapple Chutney (recipe pictured) and Citrus Slaw (recipe pictured).
3. Close up the sandwich and enjoy!

CITRUS SLAW

Ditch the heavy mayo slaw and try this light and crunchy Citrus Slaw. It works great on any pulled pork sandwich or as a side to your BBQ dishes.

1 poblano pepper
1/2 head red cabbage, thinly sliced
1/2 head green cabbage, thinly sliced
1/4 red onion, thinly sliced

6 scallions, chopped, dark green parts only
1 jalapeño, diced, seeds and ribs removed (leave them in for more spice)
2 tablespoons chopped fresh cilantro

DRESSING

3 tablespoons rice wine vinegar
2 tablespoons sugar

2 tablespoons soy sauce
1/4 cup extra virgin olive oil

1. Roast a poblano pepper over the flame on a gas range until all sides are charred. Place it in a bowl and cover with plastic wrap for 10 minutes. Using a paper towel, remove the charred skin, stem, and seeds. Dice it and place in a large mixing bowl.

2. Add red and green cabbages, onion, scallions, jalapeño, and cilantro to the bowl. Mix to combine.

3. In a small bowl, whisk together the dressing ingredients. Chill in the refrigerator.

4. Toss the vegetables with the dressing just before serving.

PRO TIPS:

- Once the slaw has been dressed, the slaw should be served immediately so it stays crunchy.

- If you don't have a gas range, you can also char the poblano under the broiler, turning every 5 minutes or so until all sides are charred.

KALUA PORK QUESADILLAS

1 tablespoon oil or butter
6 large tortillas
8 ounces grated cheddar, Mexican blend, Oaxaca, or Monterrey Jack cheese, divided

Kalua Pork (see page 54)
Pineapple Chutney (see below) or Pineapple Salsa (see page 144), for serving

1. Preheat a griddle to medium heat and add oil or butter.

2. Place a tortilla in the pan and sprinkle grated cheese over the tortilla.

3. Add shredded Kalua Pork to half of the tortilla and cook for 3–4 minutes until the tortilla starts to get golden brown and cheese begins to melt.

4. Flip the half of the tortilla without the pork onto the other half, pressing down. Continue to cook until pork is warm throughout and cheese is melted, about 2 additional minutes. If needed, use a cover over the quesadilla to melt the cheese faster.

5. Serve with Pineapple Chutney or Pineapple Salsa.

PINEAPPLE CHUTNEY

This Pineapple Chutney is sweet and tangy—a great addition to chicken, pork, or shrimp!

2 cups pineapple, diced
1/2 red bell pepper, diced, seeds and ribs removed
1/2 jalapeño, diced, seeds and ribs removed (leave them in for more spice)
1 shallot, diced
3 tablespoons brown sugar

2 tablespoons apple cider vinegar
1 tablespoon chipotle pepper in adobo sauce
1 tablespoon ginger, grated
1 clove of garlic, minced
2 tablespoons chopped fresh cilantro
1/2 tablespoon kosher salt
2 cups water

1. Add pineapple, bell pepper, jalapeño, shallot, brown sugar, apple cider vinegar, adobo sauce, ginger, garlic, cilantro, and salt to a blender. Pulse 10–15 times until chunky.

2. Pour into a saucepan over medium heat and add water; stir to combine. Bring to a boil and reduce to a simmer. Simmer for 45–60 minutes, until all ingredients are soft and flavors are developed.

3. Place in an airtight container and refrigerate until ready to use, for at least 1 hour.

APPLE CIDER-BRINED PORK TENDERLOIN WITH MANGO SALSA

Serves 4–6
Prep Time: 15 minutes
Marinade Time: 2 hours
Cook Time: 20 minutes
Total Time: 2 hours, 35 minutes

This was the recipe I made in my first live appearance on *Good Morning America!* It was a couple's cook-off and the hosts, along with Ayesha Curry, tasted both dishes and declared my recipe the winner! What an amazing experience!

BRINE

4 cups apple cider
5 peppercorns
1 teaspoon coriander seeds
1 teaspoon fennel seeds
1/2 teaspoon mustard seeds

1/4 cup brown sugar
2 bay leaves
2 tablespoons kosher salt
4 cups ice

2 pork tenderloins (1 1/2 pounds each)
1/2 teaspoon kosher salt
1/4 teaspoon black pepper

Sea salt to finish (optional)
Mango Salsa (see page 145)

1. Start the brine; in a saucepan on the stove, add apple cider, peppercorns, coriander seeds, fennel seeds, mustard seeds, brown sugar, bay leaves, and salt. Bring to a boil and then reduce to a simmer until the sugar and salt have dissolved; remove from heat. Add ice and allow to cool completely.

2. Add pork tenderloins to a ziplock bag and place the bag in a large bowl. Carefully pour the cooled brine into the bag with the pork tenderloins. Seal the bag and place the bowl in the refrigerator for at least 2 hours, or up to 6 hours.

3. Remove the pork from the brine and pat completely dry with paper towels; no need to rinse. Season with both salt and pepper.

4. Preheat the grill to medium-low heat, about 350 degrees.

5. Spray the grill grates with non-stick spray and place the pork tenderloins on the grill. Close the lid and grill for 5 minutes. Continue turning and grilling every 4 minutes until pork is cooked through. Depending on the size, this may take 15–20 minutes or until pork reaches 140 degrees.

6. When the pork is done, bring it inside and tent it with foil for 5–10 minutes to rest. Carve into 1/2-inch slices on a bias.

7. Finish with a sprinkle of sea salt. Serve with Mango Salsa.

Serves 6
Prep Time: 30 minutes
Marinade Time: 6 hours
Cook Time: 2 hours
Total Time: 8 hours, 30 minutes

PORK AL PASTOR

I love pork al pastor tacos! The flavors that hit in one bite are amazing! This was the closest way I came up with to get that slow-roasted al pastor flavor on a home smoker.

3 pounds boneless pork shoulder
1 pineapple, sliced into 1/2-inch slices
Kosher salt to taste
12 street taco–sized corn or flour tortillas

1/2 yellow onion, diced, for garnish
1/2 cup chopped fresh cilantro, for garnish
Lime wedges, for garnish

MARINADE

2 guajillo dried chiles
2 Anaheim dried chiles
2 dried chiles de árbol
1 1/2 cups pineapple juice
1 chipotle pepper in adobo sauce, plus 1 tablespoon of the chipotle sauce
5 cloves of garlic
1/2 cup fresh cilantro
1 tablespoon ground cumin

1 tablespoon ground coriander
1 tablespoon dried oregano
1/2 tablespoon smoked paprika
3 tablespoons sherry vinegar
1/2 lime, juiced
1 1/2 tablespoons kosher salt
1/2 tablespoon black pepper
1/4 cup vegetable oil

1. Slice the pork shoulder into 1/2-inch slices, or ask your butcher to slice it for you.

2. Bring a small pot of water to a boil; add the dried guajillo, Anaheim, and chile de árbol peppers. Cover and turn off the heat; steep for 20 minutes. When they are soft, remove stems and seeds.

3. In a blender, combine rehydrated chiles and the remaining marinade ingredients. Blend on high until smooth.

4. Add pork slices to a large dish or ziplock bag and coat with the marinade, reserving 1/2 cup of the marinade. Marinate for 6 hours or overnight, if possible.

5. Preheat the smoker to 350 degrees and remove the pork from the refrigerator for 30 minutes to allow to come to room temperature.

6. Dip 2 slices of pineapple in the pork marinade.

7. On a small vertical skewer/spit with a tray underneath, stack pork slices and top with the marinated 2 slices of pineapple.

8. Smoke the pork al pastor for about 2 hours, until it reaches 140 degrees. During the last 10 minutes, add additional pineapple slices to the smoker, directly on the grills. Cook for 5 minutes on each side.

9. Remove the pork and slice it down the sides in thin slices. Toss it with some of the reserved marinade and taste for seasoning; add salt if needed.

10. Chop the grilled pineapple into small chunks.

11. Serve on tortillas with smoked pineapple, onions, cilantro, and lime wedges.

PRO TIP:

- If you have a rotisserie on your grill, you can use that instead of a vertical spit, just place a tray under the pork to catch the drippings.

BEEF & LAMB

Serves 4–6
Prep Time: 10 minutes
Cook Time: 1 hour, 5 minutes
Total Time: 1 hour, 15 minutes

RIBEYE STEAKS WITH HORSERADISH GORGONZOLA SAUCE

This method of cooking steaks is my all-time favorite! At our house, we do "Friday night, steak night," so we have tried a lot of different methods. "Sous vide" translates to "under vacuum" and is a technique to bring your steak to the exact temperature you are aiming to achieve from center to edge. Then the steaks are dried completely with paper towels, and a high heat sear finishes them off to be the best steakhouse-steak-at-home you've ever had!

4 ribeye steaks
Kosher salt
Black pepper
4 sprigs fresh rosemary, divided
8 sprigs fresh thyme, divided

8 cloves of garlic, smashed, divided
2 tablespoons extra virgin olive oil, divided
Fleur de sel, for garnish
Chopped chives, for garnish

HORSERADISH GORGONZOLA SAUCE

1/2 cup heavy cream
4 ounces gorgonzola cheese, whole, broken into
    pieces

1 tablespoon prepared horseradish
1/2 teaspoon kosher salt
1/4 teaspoon black pepper

1. In a large pot of water, attach sous vide circulator and set to 125 degrees.

2. Prepare the steaks by patting dry and then adding salt and pepper to all sides.

3. Using FoodSaver BPA-free bags, add 1 steak, 1 sprig of rosemary, 2 sprigs of thyme, 2 cloves of garlic, and 1/2 tablespoon olive oil to each bag. Vacuum seal each bag, add to the water bath, and sous vide for 1–4 hours.

4. Remove steaks from sous vide, discard herbs and garlic, and pat completely dry.

5. Preheat grill to medium-high.

6. Sear steaks on both sides then turn with tongs to sear the sides, rest them loosely tented with tin foil.

7. In a small saucepan, combine the horseradish gorgonzola sauce ingredients over medium heat. Bring to a low simmer and simmer for about 10 minutes until reduced and slightly thickened.

8. Sprinkle the steaks with fleur de sel and serve with a dollop of the sauce and chopped chives.

PRO TIPS:

- This recipe is for medium-rare steaks, about 2-inches thick. With this method, the internal temperature will end up 135 degrees after resting. If you like your steaks done less or more, you will need to adjust the sous vide temperature up or down accordingly, or sear slightly longer.

- If you don't have a sous vide circulator, you can also grill the steaks, searing and then moving to indirect heat to reach your desired doneness.

- Instead of a FoodSaver vacuum sealer, you can also use another non-plastic, BPA-free bag, such as a Stasher silicone bag, sealing it completely except for one corner as you lower it into the water to force the air out and then seal it completely.

BEEF & CHORIZO CHILI

I have made this chili recipe for years; the chorizo adds a great kick of spice and really takes it to the next level. And, yes, I like beans in my chili!

3 tablespoons extra virgin olive oil, divided
1 yellow onion, diced
5 cloves of garlic, minced
2 tablespoons chili powder
1/2 tablespoon oregano
1 tablespoon cumin
1/2 tablespoon coriander
1/2 tablespoon smoked paprika
1 tablespoon kosher salt
1 teaspoon black pepper
2 tablespoons tomato paste
1 chipotle in adobo, chopped
1 cup red wine to deglaze, optional
1 pound ground beef
1 pound ground chorizo
1 can (28 ounces) crushed San Marzano tomatoes

1 can (15 ounces) tomatoes, diced
2 bay leaves
2 cups beef broth, plus more if needed
2 cans (14 ounces each) dark red kidney beans
1/2 cinnamon stick
Diced avocados, for serving
Chopped fresh cilantro, for serving
Sliced scallions, for serving
Shredded cheddar cheese, for serving
Lime wedges, for serving
Sour cream, for serving
Corn chips, for serving

Serves 6–8
Prep Time: 15 minutes
Cook Time: 1 hour
Total Time: 1 hour, 15 minutes

1. Preheat smoker to 350 degrees.

2. Heat a large Dutch oven to medium heat. Add 2 tablespoons extra virgin olive oil and onion and sauté for 5–7 minutes until translucent. Add garlic and sauté 1 more minute.

3. Add chili powder, oregano, cumin, coriander, smoked paprika, salt, and pepper. Stir to combine and allow the spices to toast and become fragrant.

4. Add tomato paste, stir to combine and cook for 2–3 minutes over medium heat. Add chopped chipotle in adobo, stir to combine. If desired, deglaze with 1 cup of red wine, bring to a boil, reduce to a simmer for 2–3 minutes.

5. Heat a separate skillet over medium heat. Add 1 tablespoon olive oil and the ground beef and chorizo. Cook about 8–10 minutes, breaking it up with a wooden spoon, until it is cooked through. Strain the fat and discard. Add the meat mixture to the Dutch oven.

6. Add the tomatoes, bay leaves, and beef broth; bring to a boil and then reduce to a simmer over low heat.

7. Drain, rinse, and add beans to the chili. Add cinnamon stick; stir to combine and then turn off the heat.

8. Transfer the pot to the smoker and smoke for 1 hour. Check on it about halfway through to skim any fat that has risen to the surface. Add more stock if needed for desired consistency.

9. Remove bay leaves and cinnamon stick. Serve with toppings such as avocados, cilantro, scallions, cheddar cheese, lime wedges, sour cream, and corn chips. Taste for seasoning, add more salt if needed.

Serves 6–8
Prep Time: 15 minutes
Cook Time: 1 hour, 30 minutes
Total Time: 1 hour, 45 minutes

SMOKED MEATBALLS

On Food Network's *The Great Food Truck Race* in Alaska, our team was the Meatball Mamas! Needless to say, I did not have a smoker on board the truck, but this was the same recipe we served all over Alaska as we competed on the show. It was an amazing experience I'll never forget, but I hope to never be as cold!

Homemade Marinara (see page 149)
1 pound 80/20 ground beef
1 pound ground pork or sausage
1/2 pound ground veal
2 cloves of garlic, grated on a microplane
1/2 tablespoon dried Italian seasoning
1 tablespoon chopped fresh basil, plus more for garnish
1 tablespoon chopped fresh parsley, plus more for garnish
1/2 tablespoon kosher salt

1/2 teaspoon black pepper
1 egg
1/4 cup grated Parmesan cheese, plus more for serving
1/4 cup panko bread crumbs
1/4 cup water
2 tablespoons extra virgin olive oil
Pasta, for serving
Chopped fresh basil, for garnish
Parsley, for garnish

1. Preheat the smoker to 400 degrees.

2. Heat the marinara sauce in a saucepan on the stove over a low simmer.

3. In a large bowl, combine the ground beef, ground pork (or sausage), ground veal, garlic, Italian seasoning, basil, parsley, salt, pepper, egg, Parmesan cheese, bread crumbs, and water. Use your hands to mix thoroughly until combined.

4. Spray a baking rack with non-stick spray and place it onto a baking sheet. Using a small ice cream scoop and your hands, form the meatballs and then place them onto the baking rack. Once they are all formed, drizzle the meatballs with olive oil.

5. Smoke for 20 minutes.

6. When they're finished, add them to the marinara and cook for 10–15 more minutes. Serve over pasta. Garnish with Parmesan cheese, basil, and parsley.

PRO TIP:

- For a weeknight shortcut, heat up your favorite jarred marinara sauce.

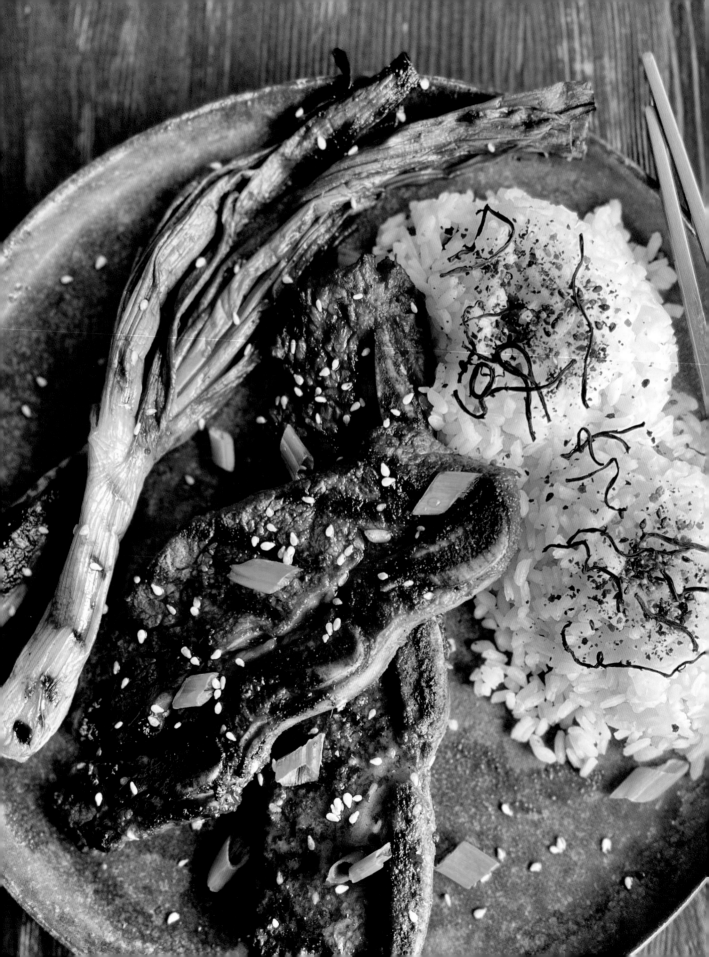

HAWAIIAN-STYLE KALBI SHORT RIBS

Serves 4
Prep Time: 15 minutes
Marinade Time: 2 hours
Cook Time: 10 minutes
Total Time: 2 hours, 25 minutes

This is a recipe that takes me straight back to my childhood in Hawaii with visions of "plate lunch." It's a quick recipe, bursting with huge flavors of the islands.

3 pounds thinly sliced short ribs, flanken style

4–6 spring onions

MARINADE

1/2 cup soy sauce

1/3 cup dark brown sugar

3 tablespoons mirin

1 tablespoon rice vinegar

1 tablespoon sriracha

3 cloves of garlic

1 tablespoon sesame seeds, for garnish

Furikake seasoning (optional)

1-inch piece of ginger, peeled and cut into cubes

1/2 cup water

1 tablespoon sesame oil

1 bunch scallions, chopped, white and light green parts, reserve dark green parts for garnish

1. Place ribs in a large baking dish.

2. In a blender, combine the soy sauce, brown sugar, mirin, rice vinegar, sriracha, garlic, ginger, and water. Blend on high until smooth.

3. Transfer to a bowl and stir in sesame oil and the white and light green scallions. Reserve 1/4 cup of the marinade for serving.

4. Add marinade to the ribs, coating all sides, and cover the dish with plastic wrap. Marinate at least 2 hours, but preferably overnight.

5. When ready to grill, bring the ribs to room temperature for 30–60 minutes, turning the ribs one more time in the marinade.

6. Add the spring onions to the marinated ribs; mix to coat the onions in the marinade and then preheat the grill to medium-high.

7. Grill the short ribs over direct heat for 4–5 minutes per side. Add the spring onions to the side of the grill over indirect heat and turn every few minutes.

8. Serve ribs garnished with sesame seeds, chopped dark green scallions, spring onions, and reserved marinade.

CHEESY SMASHBURGERS

Griddled smashburgers kind of took on a life of their own this year. I mean, I'm not arguing . . . how can you go wrong with maximizing those crispy, caramelized edges of the meat and then topping them with melty American cheese?

3 pounds 80/20 ground chuck
2 tablespoons vegetable oil
1 yellow onion, sliced
1 tablespoon of your favorite rub (kosher salt and black pepper as an alternative)

12 slices American cheese
1–2 tablespoons extra virgin olive oil
6 brioche buns, split
1 head iceberg lettuce, shredded
Sliced pickles, for serving

SAUCE

2 tablespoons mayo
2 tablespoons ketchup

2 tablespoons mustard
1 tablespoon pickle relish

1. Roll ground chuck into 12 golf ball–sized balls and set aside.

2. Combine the sauce ingredients in a small bowl.

3. Preheat griddle to medium-high and oil the surface with the vegetable oil.

4. Add small mounds of sliced onions to the griddle; then add the meat on top of the onions. Place parchment paper on the meat and press down for a few seconds; release and remove the parchment. Sprinkle with your favorite rub. Continue until all burgers have been smashed. Cook for 4–5 minutes until nicely seared.

5. Flip the burgers and add two slices of cheese to each burger. Tent with foil or cover with a domed lid. Cook for another 4–5 minutes until cheese is melted and meat is cooked through.

6. Drizzle olive oil on the inside of each top and bottom bun and set on the side of the griddle over indirect heat until toasted.

7. Add lettuce to the bottom of the bun and top it with 2 smashburger patties, pickles, sauce, the top bun. Enjoy!

STEAK FAJITAS

Serves 4–6
Prep Time: 15 minutes
Marinade Time: 6 hours
Cook Time: 15 minutes
Total Time: 6 hours, 30 minutes

Who doesn't love steak fajitas, piled high with seared peppers and onions? A quick and easy cook for the perfect family-style meal!

MARINADE

1 chipotle pepper in adobo sauce
3 tablespoons soy sauce
5 cloves of garlic
1 tablespoon cumin
1 tablespoon coriander
1/2 tablespoon oregano

1/2 lime, juiced
1/2 orange, juiced
1/2 yellow onion, roughly chopped
1/2 cup fresh cilantro, roughly chopped
1/4 cup vegetable oil

2 pounds flank or skirt steak
1 red bell pepper, thinly sliced
1 orange bell pepper, thinly sliced
1 yellow bell pepper, thinly sliced
1/2 red onion, thinly sliced
1–2 tablespoons vegetable oil
1 teaspoon sea salt (optional)

Warm tortillas, flour or corn, for serving
Queso fresco, crumbled, or cheese of preference, for serving
Guacamole, for serving
Lime wedges, for serving
Fresh cilantro, chopped, for serving

1. In a high-speed blender, combine the marinade ingredients. Blend on high speed until smooth.

2. Poke the steak a few times on both sides with a fork to allow the marinade to penetrate. Pour the marinade over the steak, reserving 1/4 cup for the vegetables. Lay the steak flat in the refrigerator and marinate 6–24 hours. Flip the bag over halfway through the marinading process.

3. Add bell peppers, onion, and reserved marinade to a medium bowl and toss to coat.

4. Bring the steak out of the refrigerator 30–45 minutes before grilling and preheat the griddle to high.

5. Add vegetable oil to the griddle and, letting the excess marinade drip off first, place the steak on the griddle. Cook for about 5 minutes until steak has a nice sear; flip, and cook another 5 minutes or so. For medium-rare, cook it until the internal temperature reaches 125 degrees. Place it on a cutting board, tented with foil, to rest. Sprinkle with sea salt.

6. While the steak is cooking, add the vegetables to the other side of the griddle. Cook 2–3 minutes, turn, and continue cooking another 5 minutes or so until slightly charred and softened. Remove vegetables to a platter.

7. Check the steak to see which way the grain runs and slice thinly in 1/4-inch strips against the grain—this will create a more tender bite of steak.

8. Serve with warm tortillas, queso fresco, guacamole, lime wedges, and cilantro.

Serves 4
Prep Time: 5 minutes
Cook Time: 15 minutes
Total Time: 20 minutes

ZA'ATAR GRILLED RACK OF LAMB

I was born in New Zealand, so my love of lamb runs deep. We always have a leg of lamb for Easter and Christmas Eve. For a quicker cook that's just as flavorful, a rack of lamb is a special treat! Za'atar is a Middle Eastern spice blend that brings out incredible flavor in the lamb. If you haven't tried it or cooked with it before, now's a great time!

2 tablespoons za'atar
1 1/2 teaspoons onion powder
1 1/2 teaspoons garlic powder
2 cloves of garlic, minced
1 teaspoon kosher salt

1/2 teaspoon black pepper
2 tablespoons extra virgin olive oil
2 8-bone racks of lamb
Sea salt (optional)

1. In a small bowl, combine the za'atar, onion powder, garlic powder, garlic, salt, and pepper. Add olive oil and stir to make a paste.

2. Rub the paste on all sides of both racks of lamb.

3. Preheat the grill to medium, about 425 degrees. If you have a heat-safe thermometer probe, such as a Meater, insert it horizontally into the middle of the lamb chops.

4. Spray the grill with non-stick spray. Sear the racks, meat-side down, for 3 minutes until grill marks are achieved. Stand the racks up on the cap side to sear them for 2 minutes. Flip racks bone-side down, lower the heat to low, and continue to cook until the internal temperature reaches 125 degrees for medium-rare. Remove to a platter and loosely tent with foil. Temperature will continue to rise for another 5 degrees or so while they rest.

5. Carve into one or two bone chops and sprinkle with sea salt to finish.

KICKED-UP SLOPPY JOES

Serves 6
Prep Time: 10 minutes
Cook Time: 40 minutes
Total Time: 50 minutes

Taking an old classic (no offense if you grew up in the '70s or '80s) and reinventing it to kick it up with a little hint of smoky spice. All the flavors you know and love with my own twist.

3–5 tablespoons extra virgin olive oil, divided
1/2 onion, diced
1 teaspoon kosher salt
1/2 teaspoon black pepper

3 cloves of garlic, minced
3 tablespoons tomato paste
2 pounds ground beef
12 hamburger buns

SEASONING

1 tablespoon chili powder
1 teaspoon dry mustard
1 tablespoon onion powder
1 tablespoon garlic powder

1 teaspoon smoked paprika
1/4 teaspoon cayenne
1 tablespoon kosher salt
1 teaspoon black pepper

SAUCE

1 cup ketchup
3 tablespoons brown sugar
1 tablespoon Worcestershire sauce

1/4 cup apple cider vinegar
2 tablespoons chipotle peppers in adobo sauce
1/3 cup water

1. Preheat smoker to 375 degrees.

2. Heat a large skillet with deep sides over medium heat. Add 1–2 tablespoons olive oil. Add onion, salt, and pepper and sauté for 5–7 minutes until translucent. Add garlic and cook 1 more minute.

3. Combine the seasoning ingredients in a bowl.

4. Add the seasoning and tomato paste to the skillet and cook 1–2 minutes until fragrant. Make a spot in the middle of the skillet and add the ground beef, breaking it up with a wooden spoon and stirring to combine the meat with the onions, garlic, and spices. Continue to cook until meat is cooked through, another 8 minutes or so, and then turn off the heat.

5. Combine the sauce ingredients in a bowl.

6. Add the sauce to the skillet and stir to combine.

7. Place the skillet on the smoker and smoke for 20–30 minutes until sauce has thickened and meat has a touch of smoky flavor.

8. Drizzle the buns with 2–3 tablespoons olive oil and toast. Serve sloppy joes on toasted buns.

Serves 4
Prep Time: 10 minutes
Cook Time: 15 minutes
Total Time: 25 minutes

LOADED PHILLY CHEESESTEAKS

When my husband and I started dating, he asked me what I wanted for dinner one night, to which I responded, "Something light, like a Philly cheesesteak." I'm still not sure, to this day, how or why that came out of my mouth, but it made perfect sense to me at the time! It was at that moment he knew he wanted to marry me. True story.

2 pounds ribeye steaks
3 tablespoons vegetable oil, divided
1 yellow onion, thinly sliced
2 cups button mushrooms, thinly sliced
1 1/2 tablespoons kosher salt, divided
2 teaspoons black pepper, divided

1 tablespoon extra virgin olive oil
4 hoagie rolls, split
12 slices provolone, thinly sliced
Sweet and hot peppers, thinly sliced, for garnish (optional)

1. Slice the ribeye steaks very thin, about 1/4-inch thick, against the grain.

2. Preheat the griddle to high on one side and medium-low on the other side.

3. Add 1 1/2 tablespoons vegetable oil to the medium-low side of the griddle surface. Add onions and mushrooms; then add 1/2 tablespoon salt and 1 teaspoon pepper to onions and mushrooms. Cook for about 10 minutes until the onions are translucent and the mushrooms begin to brown. Once cooked, remove to a bowl for serving.

4. Add olive oil to the hoagie rolls and place face-side down on the medium-low side to toast.

5. Add 1 1/2 tablespoons vegetable oil to the griddle side on high and add the steak in a single layer. Sprinkle with 1 tablespoon salt and 1 teaspoon pepper. Let the meat sear for 1–2 minutes; then use a large metal spatula to flip the meat to the other side. Allow to sear another 1–2 minutes.

6. Using the large metal spatula, begin to chop up the ribeye steak into small pieces; flip to continue cooking.

7. Form the meat into a long formation, similar size to the buns. Cover all the meat with provolone cheese slices. Tent with foil or cover with a dome lid without touching the cheese.

8. Place the toasted bun on top of the meat and melted cheese and use your spatula to scoop up all the meat into the bun.

9. Top with sautéed onions, mushrooms, and sweet and hot peppers.

PRO TIP:

- Ask your butcher to slice the ribeye for you.

LEMONGRASS BEEF CUPS

This recipe was inspired by my sister-in-law, Lisa. She and her mom came over one day to make their family recipe for lemongrass pork; it was so flavorful, one of the best dishes I've ever tasted! I was so inspired by the Vietnamese flavors, I wanted to include it in my cookbook in the form of beef skewers. This recipe can be made with beef, pork, or chicken, and the flavors will blow you away!

MARINADE

2 stalks lemongrass, tough outer leaves removed to reveal the tender inner core

3 cloves of garlic, roughly chopped

1 lime, zested and juiced

1/4 cup fish sauce

2 tablespoons soy sauce

2 tablespoons brown sugar

1/2 teaspoon black pepper

4 scallions, chopped, white and light green parts, reserve dark green parts for serving

1 teaspoon Chinese five spice

2 tablespoons vegetable oil

1 tablespoon sesame oil

SAUCE

3 tablespoons rice vinegar

2 tablespoons white sugar

1/2 lime, juiced

1 tablespoon fish sauce

1/4 cup warm water

1 tablespoon spicy chili crisp (optional)

1 1/2 pounds skirt steak

1 package mung bean threads, prepared to package directions

1 head Bibb lettuce, cleaned and leaves separated

1 carrot, julienned thinly into 3-inch segments

1 English or Persian cucumber, julienned thinly into 3-inch segments

Fresh mint leaves, for serving

Fresh Thai basil leaves, for serving

Fresh cilantro, for serving

1. In a blender, combine the marinade ingredients. Blend until smooth.

2. Thinly slice the steak against the grain. If it is a long piece of steak, it helps to cut it in half first.

3. In a large baking dish, add the steak and pour the marinade over the top; toss to combine completely. Cover and place in the refrigerator to marinate for 6 hours or overnight.

4. Preheat the grill to medium-high and bring out the steak to rest at room temperature.

5. Combine the sauce ingredients in a small bowl. Stir until the sugar is dissolved and then set aside to let the flavors marry.

6. Skewer the steak in a zigzag pattern, folding every inch or so. You should be able to fit about 3 slices of steak on each skewer, sliding together, but allowing a little space for heat to travel between.

7. Grill the skewers so they get a char on all sides, 5 minutes per side.

8. Serve family-style with skewers and all the additions to build your own lettuce cups: mung bean noodles, carrots, cucumbers, dark green scallions, reserved sauce, basil, and cilantro.

PRO TIP:

- If you're using wooden skewers, be sure to soak them in water for at least 1 hour prior to grilling.

SMOKED BEEF RIBS

You know the kinds of meals that you wake up thinking about the next morning? Yeah, this is that meal. The "king" of all ribs, in my humble opinion, is this tender, meaty beef rib!

1–2 racks of beef plate ribs
3–4 tablespoons Worcestershire sauce
Prime rib or steak seasoning of choice, such as Meat Church Holy Cow BBQ Rub

Spritzes of equal parts apple cider vinegar and water
Wagyu beef tallow, a few tablespoons per rack of ribs

1. Preheat the smoker to 250 degrees.

2. Rub all sides of the ribs with Worcestershire sauce. Coat all sides with prime rib or steak seasoning. Place a heat-proof probe, such as a Meater thermometer, into the center of the meat so it's not touching any bones.

3. Smoke the ribs for 1 hour. After 1 hour, begin spritzing them with diluted apple cider vinegar once every hour.

4. Smoke ribs until they hit about 170 degrees. This should take about 3 hours. Remove the ribs and thermometer. Increase smoker temperature to 275 degrees.

5. Overlap 2 sheets of butcher paper, spread some Wagyu beef tallow to the middle of the butcher paper, place the ribs, meat-side down on top of the beef tallow, spritz one last time with apple cider vinegar, and wrap tight. Insert the thermometer into the center of the meat once again.

6. Place the tightly wrapped ribs back on the smoker and cook for an additional 3–5 hours or until internal temperature reaches about 203 degrees.

7. When the ribs are done, leave them tightly wrapped and put them in an airtight cooler, like a Yeti. I always put a towel down on the bottom and place the wrapped ribs on top. After they've rested for 1 hour, cut them into ribs to serve.

PRO TIP:

- Membrane removal from the backside of the bones is optional. I tend to leave it on because it does help keep the bones intact.

SEAFOOD

Serves 4
Prep time: 10 minutes
Marinade Time: 1 hour
Cook time: 20 minutes
Total time: 1 hour, 30 minutes

CHILEAN SEA BASS EN PAPILLOTE

Cooking *en papillote* means to cook in paper. It's a great method for fish because it steams it perfectly with all the ingredients together and it turns out beautifully flaky and delicious!

4 sea bass fillets (6–7 ounces each, about 1 1/2–2 inches thick)

2–3 tablespoons light miso paste

4 baby bok choy, cleaned and sliced vertically in half

1 red bell pepper, thinly sliced vertically, seeds removed

1 cup shitake mushrooms, thinly sliced

1 shallot, thinly sliced

1 red Fresno chili, thinly sliced, seeds removed

Jasmine rice, steamed, for serving

SAUCE

1/4 cup soy sauce

1 tablespoon hoisin sauce

1 tablespoon sriracha

2 tablespoons rice vinegar

3 tablespoons water

4 cloves of garlic, minced

1 tablespoon ginger, grated

3 tablespoons sesame oil

3 scallions, sliced, white and light green parts, reserve dark green parts for garnish

1. Brush fish with light miso paste and marinate for a minimum of 1 hour, but up to 24 hours.

2. Preheat the smoker to 375 degrees.

3. Combine the sauce ingredients and set aside.

4. In a large bowl, stir together the bok choy, bell pepper, mushrooms, shallots, and Fresno chili. Divide the vegetables into fourths.

5. Take 4 large, square pieces of parchment paper and lay them on the counter.

6. For each packet, place the vegetables in a small mound slightly right of center. Place the sea bass in the center of the vegetables and spoon a few tablespoons of the sauce over the fish and vegetables. Reserve the remainder of the sauce for serving.

7. Fold the parchment paper over the fish and vegetables like a book so the edges line up. Beginning at the top left corner, begin folding and pinching the paper all around the fish. When you get to the end of the parchment paper, tuck it under the whole packet so you create a sealed packet all the way around that leaves room for steam to pass around.

8. Carefully place the packet on a baking sheet.

9. Continue with all the pieces of fish until they are all lined up on the baking sheet.

10. Place the baking sheet of fish packets on the smoker and cook for 15–20 minutes, depending on the thickness of the fish.

11. Remove and carefully open the packets to let the steam escape. Serve the fish and vegetables on a plate with steamed jasmine rice, spooning some of the reserved sauce over top and garnishing with dark green scallions.

PRO TIP:

• A good rule of thumb for cooking fish is 10 minutes of cooking time for every inch of thickness.

MIXED SEAFOOD PAELLA

There's nothing better than a huge pan of paella to feed a crowd. You can add all kinds of ingredients, depending on what you feel like. This is my favorite combo, which includes spicy andouille sausage and a whole bunch of mixed seafood. The flavors of this dish are unreal!

4 cups chicken or seafood stock

1 teaspoon saffron threads

2 tablespoons extra virgin olive oil, plus 1–2 tablespoons more if needed

6 ounces andouille sausage in casing (linguica or another spicy sausage as an alternative)

1 small yellow onion, diced

2 cloves of garlic, minced

1 tablespoon cumin

1 tablespoon pimentón or smoked paprika

1/2 tablespoon oregano

2 tablespoons tomato paste

2 cups paella rice, such as bomba, or a short grain rice

1/4 cup dry white wine

1 can (28 ounces) diced tomatoes

4 teaspoons kosher salt, divided

1 1/2 teaspoons black pepper, divided

10 mussels

10 clams

12 large shrimp, peeled and deveined, leaving the tail intact

1 lobster tail, cut down the back of the shell, laying the meat on top of its shell, tail intact

1/4 cup green peas at room temperature

1 lemon, cut into wedges, for garnish

1. Preheat smoker to 400 degrees.

2. In a small saucepan, add chicken stock and saffron. Bring to a simmer to dissolve saffron in the broth, about 10 minutes. Turn off and set aside.

3. Heat a flat-bottomed, low-rimmed paella pan to medium heat and add olive oil. Add sliced andouille sausage and cook about 2 minutes per side until golden brown. Remove to a plate until needed.

4. In the same pan, over medium-low heat, add onions and sauté until softened, about 5–7 minutes. Add garlic and sauté 1 more minute. Add cumin, pimentón, oregano, and tomato paste; stir to combine.

5. Add rice to the pan and stir to combine with the other ingredients. Add 1–2 more tablespoons olive oil if it looks dry.

6. Add white wine and cook off for 1 minute. Then add saffron broth, tomatoes, 3 teaspoons salt, and 1 teaspoon pepper. Stir to combine.

7. Place the paella on the smoker, close the lid, and do not stir for the remainder of the cooking process. Smoke paella for 25 minutes.

8. Soak the mussels and clams in a bowl of cold water for about 20 minutes.

9. Season the shrimp and lobster tails with 1 teaspoon salt and 1/2 teaspoon pepper.

10. Increase smoker to 425 degrees. Place the mussels and clams throughout the paella, tucking the seams well into the liquid so they can cook and open. Next, add the andouille sausage

and shrimp. Place the lobster tail on top. Close the lid and smoke 20–25 minutes until seafood is cooked through and mussels and clams have opened. Discard any that have not opened.

11. Sprinkle the peas on top, close the lid for 1 minute to heat through, then remove. Garnish with lemon wedges.

PRO TIPS:

- This recipe can also be made inside on the stovetop; cooking times remain the same.
- If mussels and clams are slow to open, you can place a sheet of aluminum foil over them for a couple minutes to see if more will open.

LEMON & HERB CEDAR PLANK SALMON

Serves 4
Prep Time: 10 minutes
Marinade Time: 10 minutes
Cook Time: 45 minutes
Total Time: 1 hour, 5 minutes

Cedar plank salmon is another cooking method to ensure a moist, flavorful result. The cedar plank adds a nice smoky flavor to the salmon; add a squeeze of lemon over the top, and it's perfection!

1 Cedar plank
2 pounds salmon fillet

1/2 lemon, thinly sliced
Fresh dill, chopped, for garnish (optional)

MARINADE

1/2 tablespoon lemon pepper
1 clove of garlic, minced
1 teaspoon dry Italian seasoning

1 teaspoon kosher salt
1/2 lemon, zested and juiced
2 tablespoons extra virgin olive oil

1. Completely soak the cedar plank in water for at least 1 hour to avoid burning.

2. Pat salmon completely dry, remove cedar plank from water, and set salmon on the plank, skin-side down.

3. In a small bowl, whisk together the marinade ingredients until a paste is formed.

4. Cover the top and sides of the salmon with the marinade, top with lemon slices, and let sit at room temperature while the smoker preheats.

5. Preheat the smoker to 350 degrees.

6. Place the cedar plank salmon on the smoker and close the lid. Smoke salmon for 35–45 minutes, or until it reaches 135 degrees or desired doneness. Start checking the temperature after 30 minutes.

7. Remove and sprinkle with dill or another squeeze of lemon, if desired.

PRO TIP:

- Cooking time will vary based on the thickness of your salmon fillet. An instant-read thermometer or Meater probe will help to alert you when it's finished.

Serves 6
Prep Time: 30 minutes
Cook Time: 10 minutes
Total Time: 40 minutes

MAHI MAHI TACOS

Kick up Taco Tuesday with fish tacos! These Mahi Mahi Tacos are my favorite kind of fish tacos to make. Adding the crunchy slaw, the sweet pineapple salsa, and a drizzle of the chipotle crema makes for the best bite!

SLAW

1/2 head green cabbage, thinly sliced
1/2 head red cabbage, thinly sliced
3 scallions, chopped

1 jalapeño, diced, seeds and ribs removed
1/4 cup chopped fresh cilantro

CHIPOTLE CREMA

1/3 cup sour cream
1 tablespoon chipotle pepper in adobo sauce
1/2 lime, zested and juiced

1 teaspoon sugar
1 teaspoon kosher salt
1/2 teaspoon black pepper

2 pounds mahi mahi fillet, bones and skin removed
2 tablespoons Mexican Spice Rub (see page 135)
2 tablespoons vegetable oil

12 warm corn or flour tortillas
Pineapple Salsa (see page 144), keep refrigerated until ready to serve
Lime wedges, for garnish
Fresh cilantro, chopped, for garnish

1. Combine the slaw ingredients in a large bowl, cover with plastic wrap, and place in the refrigerator until ready to serve.

2. Combine the chipotle crema ingredients in a small bowl, cover with plastic wrap, and place in the refrigerator until ready to serve.

3. Preheat the griddle to medium heat.

4. Pat the mahi mahi completely dry and season all sides with the rub.

5. Add vegetable oil to the hot griddle and add the mahi mahi. Cover with a domed lid and cook for 4–5 minutes. Flip, re-cover, and cook another 4–5 minutes until fish is cooked through. Cooking time may vary depending on how thick the fish is.

6. Remove fish and cut into 1-inch strips.

7. Toss the slaw with the chipotle crema to lightly coat.

8. To serve, assemble a warm tortilla with the slaw, mahi mahi, and Pineapple Salsa. Serve with lime wedges or additional cilantro, if desired.

SWORDFISH SKEWERS WITH CHARRED MEYER LEMON GREMOLATA

Serves 4–6
Prep Time: 10 minutes
Cook Time: 10 minutes
Total Time: 25 minutes

Gremolata is an accompaniment or sauce, usually made of chopped fresh parsley, lemon zest, and garlic, although many other combinations can be used. In my version, I charred the Meyer lemons to really accentuate their sweet lemon flavor. It's light and bright and pairs perfectly with the grilled swordfish skewers!

2 pounds swordfish steaks, skin removed
2 tablespoons extra virgin olive oil, plus 1 tablespoon for drizzle when serving
2 cloves of garlic, minced

GREMOLATA
1 bunch fresh parsley, chopped
2 Meyer lemons, 1 zested and 1 halved
2 cloves of garlic, minced

1 tablespoon herbes de Provence
1 teaspoon kosher salt
1/4 teaspoon black pepper
1 Meyer lemon

2 tablespoons extra virgin olive oil
1/4 teaspoon kosher salt
1/8 teaspoon black pepper

1. Cut the swordfish steaks into 1 1/2-inch cubes.

2. Add the swordfish to a large bowl and gently toss with olive oil, garlic, herbes de Provence, salt, and pepper.

3. Preheat the grill to medium-low, about 325 degrees.

4. Slice lemon into 1/4-inch slices to make thin rounds.

5. Skewer the swordfish, adding a slice of lemon in between each piece of fish.

6. While the grill heats, create the gremolata. Combine parsley, lemon zest, garlic, olive oil, salt, and pepper in a small bowl.

7. Spray the grill grates with non-stick spray so the fish doesn't stick. Add the swordfish skewers and one lemon half to the grill and close the lid. Grill on medium-low for 4–5 minutes until grill marks are achieved. Flip the fish and grill another 4–5 minutes until it is cooked through and lemons are charred with grill marks. Remove skewers and lemons to a platter.

8. Juice the charred lemon into the gremolata; stir to combine.

9. Serve swordfish skewers on a platter with a drizzle of olive oil and gremolata.

PRO TIPS:

- If possible, use metal skewers. If using wooden skewers, be sure to soak them in water for an hour prior to grilling so they don't burn.

- This recipe goes well with Zucchini & Summer Squash Skewers (see page 124).

CHIPOTLE LIME SHRIMP BOWLS

When our daughter comes home from college, she can't wait for a home-cooked meal! Her favorite and most often requested are the bowls I put together. Everyone can build their own, so everyone is happy! These Chipotle Lime Shrimp Bowls are the perfect light dinner!

3 ears of corn
1 tablespoon vegetable oil
1 head romaine lettuce, thinly chopped
8 ounces cherry tomatoes, diced
1 avocado, diced

1 block (8 ounces) Monterrey Jack cheese, grated
1 can (15 ounces) black beans, drained and rinsed
1 bunch scallions, chopped
Pepitas, for serving

CILANTRO LIME DRESSING

1 tablespoon Dijon mustard
1 clove of garlic, minced
1 1/2 tablespoons honey
1/3 cup extra virgin olive oil
1 teaspoon kosher salt

1/2 teaspoon black pepper
1 lime, zested and half juiced
1/4 cup chopped fresh cilantro
2 tablespoons red wine vinegar
2 tablespoons water

SHRIMP CHIPOTLE MARINADE

1/2 tablespoon kosher salt
1 teaspoon black pepper
1 teaspoon smoked paprika
1 tablespoon cumin
1 teaspoon coriander
1 teaspoon dried oregano

1 tablespoon chipotle pepper in adobo sauce
3 cloves of garlic, minced
1/4 cup extra virgin olive oil
1 lime, zested and juiced
1 1/2 pounds U15 shrimp, peeled and deveined, tails left on if desired

CILANTRO LIME RICE

1 cup rice, prepared to package directions
1/2 lime, juiced

2 tablespoons chopped fresh cilantro

1. Preheat the grill to medium heat.

2. Husk corn and brush with vegetable oil; set aside.

3. Whisk the cilantro lime dressing ingredients together in a small bowl. Cover and store in the refrigerator until ready to serve.

4. In a large bowl, combine the shrimp chipotle marinade ingredients. Do not marinate the shrimp for longer than 15–20 minutes.

5. Skewer the shrimp for the grill.

6. Spray the grill with non-stick spray. Grill the shrimp and corn over medium heat. Flip the shrimp and rotate the corn after 2–3 minutes. Cook another 2–3 minutes on the other side until no longer translucent.

7. Remove shrimp from the grill and continue to grill the corn for another 5 minutes or until there are char marks on all sides. Cut the corn kernels from the cobs and place in a bowl.

8. Combine the cooked rice with the lime juice and cilantro in a bowl; stir to combine.

9. Build the bowls with grilled corn, cilantro lime rice, romaine lettuce, tomatoes, avocados, cheese, black beans, scallions, and pepitas. Top with grilled shrimp. Drizzle with dressing and serve.

PRO TIP:

- If using wooden skewers, be sure to soak them in water for at least 1 hour prior to grilling to prevent burning.

GRILLED WHOLE SNAPPER

Serves 4
Prep Time: 10 minutes
Cook Time: 20 minutes
Total Time: 30 minutes

Grilling a whole fish may seem intimidating, but it's actually very easy and makes for a great presentation. Ask the fish monger to fillet the fish, it makes it a lot easier. From there, preparing and cooking it is very easy! You can use this method with whatever fresh fish is available in your area.

2 snappers or whole white flaky fish of choice
2 lemons
1 teaspoon kosher salt, plus more to taste
1/2 teaspoon black pepper

4 sprigs parsley, divided
4 sprigs thyme, divided
1 small shallot, sliced into rounds, divided
Extra virgin olive oil to coat both sides of fish

1. Start the grill; if using a charcoal grill, lower the coals to the lowest level, if possible.

2. Cut 2–3 small 2-inch slits in the fish, parallel to each other on both sides.

3. Slice 1 lemon into rounds. Halve the other lemon end to end, cut one half into wedges.

4. Salt and pepper the fish, inside and out. Next, place 2 sprigs of parsley and 2 sprigs of thyme inside the fish. Add a few round slices of lemon and shallot on top. Tie the fish closed with butcher's twine and coat the entire fish with olive oil on all sides.

5. Brush the grill grates and spray with non-stick spray. Place the fish on the grill with the lid open and grill for approximately 10 minutes. You will notice the flesh of the fish begins to turn from translucent to opaque. Flip and cook another 10 minutes or so until this side of the flesh is also opaque. When it's ready, the internal temperature should be around 140 degrees.

6. Remove the fish and allow to rest for a few minutes.

7. Remove the twine, herbs, and lemon. Open the fish to serve; drizzle with fresh lemon, sprinkle with salt if needed, and serve with additional lemon wedges, if desired.

PRO TIP:

- If you have a fish grill basket, this will work great instead of butcher's twine.

GRILLED LOBSTER TAILS

Grilled lobster tails are so easy to prep and throw on the grill, the perfect addition to a surf n' turf night! Drizzled with garlic butter and a squeeze of lemon, there's nothing better!

4 lobster tails (6-8 oz. each)
1 tablespoon extra virgin olive oil
1/2 teaspoon kosher salt
1/4 teaspoon black pepper
2 Meyer lemons, cut in half

8 tablespoons butter, divided for brushing and
  serving
2 cloves garlic, minced
Fresh parsley, chopped for garnish, if desired

1. Heat a grill to medium heat.

2. Using sharp kitchen shears, cut the lobster tails along the back, all the way down, keeping each tail intact. Open lobster tails to lay flat. As another option, cut the lobster down the back and lift the lobster meat to set it on top of the shells. In either case, remove the large vein running down the meat.

3. Add olive oil, salt, and pepper.

4. Brush lemon halves with olive oil and add cut-side down to the grill over indirect heat.

5. Grill lobster tails, flesh side down, for 4–5 minutes.

6. Add butter and minced garlic cloves to a small, grill-safe saucepan. Place the saucepan over indirect heat to melt the butter and combine the garlic.

7. Flip lobster tails and brush with the melted garlic butter.

8. Check on the lemon halves. When they have grill marks, remove them to a platter.

9. Grill lobster tails another 3–5 minutes, until cooked through and opaque in color.

10. Remove to a platter, drizzle with remaining garlic butter, and add some chopped parsley if desired.

LOW-COUNTRY BOIL

Serves 6-8
Prep Time 15 minutes
Cook Time 20 minutes
Total Time 35 minutes

When we lived in California, we had close friends who were from Georgia, and every year they brought a little bit of the South to town by hosting a Low-Country Boil over Labor Day weekend. It was so much fun to watch them load up the huge pot with delicious ingredients and to serve it all rolled out over layers of butcher paper family style! We have carried on their tradition and now do our own Low-Country Boil with friends and family. It's a lot of fun and so full of flavor, it's so much fun!

1 packet of crab boil seasoning, such as Zatarain's

2 lemons, halved

2 bay leaves

10 cloves of garlic, smashed

1 onion, quartered into segments

8 tablespoons butter

2 cloves of garlic, minced

12 baby potatoes, gold and red

6 ears of corn, cut in half

2 pounds kielbasa or andouille sausage, cut into 3-inch segments

4 half crab sections

3 pounds large 16/20 shrimp

Cajun seasoning, if desired

1. Fill a large pot with water and add the crab boil seasoning, lemons, bay leaves, garlic cloves, and the quartered onion. Bring the mixture to a boil and reduce to a simmer.

2. In a separate small pot, add a stick of butter to melt and minced garlic.

3. Add the baby potatoes and simmer for 10 minutes. Then add the corn and sausages; simmer for 5 minutes.

4. Add the crab and shrimp, simmer for 3–4 minutes.

5. Strain everything and serve on a platter or roll out over a few sheets of butcher paper.

6. Drizzle with garlic butter and sprinkle with more Cajun seasoning if desired.

VEGGIES & SIDES

GRILLED RATATOUILLE

Serves 6–8 skewers
Prep Time: 15 minutes
Cook Time: 15 minutes
Total Time: 30 minutes

I love Grilled Ratatouille because it makes the best side dish to any of your outdoor cooking! Traditionally, ratatouille is hit with a splash of red wine vinegar toward the end of the cooking process. In my version, I drizzle a basil vinaigrette that has red wine vinegar as one of the ingredients, but the addition of basil really adds to the dish!

2 zucchinis
2 yellow summer squash
1 red bell pepper (or any color bell pepper)
1 red onion
8 large cherry tomatoes

3 tablespoons extra virgin olive oil
2 tablespoons All-Purpose Seasoning (see page 134)
Basil vinaigrette, for serving (see page 143)
1 tablespoon torn fresh basil, for garnish

1. Slice the zucchini and squash into 1/2-inch slices. Cut the bell pepper and onion into 1-inch chunks. Rinse cherry tomatoes.

2. Toss vegetables in a large bowl with olive oil and seasoning.

3. Preheat grill to medium-low. Spray with non-stick spray.

4. On a skewer, alternate stacking the vegetables tomato, zucchini, summer squash, bell pepper, and onion. Continue stacking until all vegetables are used; it should make 6–8 skewers, depending on the size.

5. Grill the skewers, rotating every 3–4 minutes. Continue grilling until all sides are grilled and vegetables are cooked through, about 15 minutes.

6. Serve on a platter. Drizzle with Basil Vinaigrette and basil. Can be served warm or at room temperature.

PRO TIPS:

- If using wooden skewers, be sure to soak them in water for 1 hour before grilling.
- Be sure to use large cherry tomatoes so they stay intact while cooking.

GREEK SALAD

Whenever I make Greek food for family, friends, or clients, I always include this Greek Salad. My Greek mother-in-law taught me the trick years ago of adding some of the kalamata olive juices into the dressing—it really gives a nice punch of flavor!

This recipe is featured with Greek-Inspired Chicken Souvlaki Skewers on page 36.

1/3 red onion
6 tomatoes of choice (Roma work well)
1 English cucumber
12 kalamata olives, pitted

DRESSING
1/2 cup extra virgin olive oil
1/4 cup red wine vinegar
2 cloves of garlic, minced
1 teaspoon kosher salt

1 tablespoon chopped fresh dill, for garnish
1 tablespoon chopped fresh oregano, for garnish
4 ounces feta cheese, diced into small cubes

1/2 teaspoon black pepper
1–2 tablespoons juice from the kalamata olives (optional)

1. Thinly slice the onion and soak in a bowl of ice water for 20 minutes. Remove and pat dry.

2. Slice the tomatoes, cucumber, and olives and add to a large bowl, along with the onions.

3. Make the dressing by whisking the ingredients in a bowl.

4. Toss the salad with the dressing and chill in the refrigerator until ready to serve.

5. To serve, add some dill and oregano and top with feta cheese.

CHEESY POTATO STACKS

Serves 6
Prep Time: 10 minutes
Cook Time: 40 minutes
Total Time: 50 minutes

This is a great side to feed a crowd. Because they are made in a muffin tin, you can cook all twelve at once! They are individual au gratin potatoes with a kiss of smoke!

1–2 Tablespoons extra virgin olive oil
2 tablespoons butter
2 tablespoons flour
2 cups heavy cream
2 cloves of garlic, grated
1/2 tablespoon kosher salt

1 teaspoon black pepper
5–6 small/medium Yukon Gold potatoes
3/4 cup Parmesan cheese, plus 2 tablespoons for serving, grated
1/2 cup Gouda cheese, grated
1 tablespoon chopped fresh chives, for garnish

1. Preheat the smoker to 375 degrees. Lightly grease a muffin tin with olive oil.

2. In a pot on the stove, heat over medium heat and add butter and flour; whisk to combine. Once combined, slowly pour in the heavy cream, whisking constantly until smooth. Add the garlic, salt, and pepper; stir to combine.

3. Once it starts to bubble, turn the heat to low and let it simmer to thicken, about 5 minutes.

4. While the sauce is simmering, thinly slice the potatoes, about 1/4-inch thick, or slice with a mandolin, and add to a large bowl.

5. Turn off the heat to the sauce and whisk in the Parmesan and Gouda cheeses until thoroughly combined.

6. Carefully pour the sauce over the potatoes. Gently use tongs to flip potatoes and ensure they are evenly coated. Then move the potatoes from the bowl to a muffin tin, along with any of the sauce that sticks. Fill each cup almost to the top. Sprinkle each of the potato stacks with Parmesan cheese.

7. Place the muffin tin on top of a baking sheet (in case there is any spillover) and place the baking sheet and muffin tin on the smoker. Smoke the potatoes for about 35–40 minutes until they are cooked through and fork tender.

8. Garnish with chives.

PRO TIPS:

* Using small to medium Yukon Gold potatoes works best, rather than the tiny baby potatoes; they will sit flatter if you choose a size that will fit nicely in the muffin tin.

* Using a mandoline is helpful for even slices, or carefully slice them by hand.

* I did not use either end of the potatoes, only the center slices for a more even stack.

Serves 6
Prep Time: 15 minutes
Cook Time: 45 minutes
Total Time: 1 hour

SMOKED GERMAN POTATO SALAD

What is a summer cookout without a potato salad? This is my version of a German potato salad, lightened up with a tangy Dijon vinaigrette instead of mayo. The flavors are BIG, and it is sure to be a hit at your next backyard BBQ!

6 slices thick-cut bacon
10 medium Yukon Gold potatoes
3 scallions, chopped, white and light green parts, reserve dark green parts for garnish

2 tablespoons chopped fresh parsley, divided
1 tablespoon chopped fresh dill, divided
Extra virgin olive oil, for drizzle garnish

DRESSING
1/2 tablespoon Dijon mustard
1/2 tablespoon whole grain mustard
3 tablespoons apple cider vinegar
1 teaspoon sugar
2 cloves of garlic, minced

1 teaspoon kosher salt
1/2 teaspoon black pepper
1/4 cup extra virgin olive oil, plus more to drizzle

1. Preheat the smoker to 400 degrees and preheat the oven to 400 degrees.

2. Use a fork to poke a few holes on each side of each potato.

3. Smoke the potatoes for about 45 minutes until they are fork tender. Halfway through smoking, turn them to the other side.

4. While the potatoes are smoking, in the oven on the middle rack, bake the bacon on a rack-lined baking sheet until crisp, about 20 minutes, flipping halfway through. Remove bacon to a paper towel–lined plate, reserving a few tablespoons of the bacon grease in a small bowl. Chop the bacon and set aside.

5. While the bacon is cooking, whisk the dressing ingredients together in a small bowl.

6. When the potatoes are done, remove them and let cool for about 10 minutes. Dice them into a medium chunks, add them to a bowl, and, while they're still warm, drizzle the dressing and reserved bacon fat over the top. Stir to combine.

7. Stir in the white and light green scallions, and half the chopped herbs and chopped bacon.

8. Garnish with the dark green scallions, remaining chopped herbs, and chopped bacon. Drizzle with olive oil and serve.

PRO TIP:

- For larger potatoes, they may require an additional 15 minutes of cook time.

CRISPY YUKON GOLD POTATOES WITH ROMESCO SAUCE

Romesco is one of my favorite sauces, but it sometimes gets forgotten. It's a tomato-based sauce that originated in Spain. It adds a bright, smoky tang to the dish!

10 small/medium Yukon Gold potatoes
2–3 tablespoons vegetable oil
1 teaspoon kosher salt

ROMESCO SAUCE
2 medium tomatoes
1 red bell pepper
3–4 tablespoons vegetable oil, divided
1 head of garlic
2 1/2 teaspoons kosher salt, divided
1 slice sourdough bread, lightly toasted

1/2 teaspoon black pepper
Fresh parsley, for garnish

1/4 cup roasted almonds
1 teaspoon pimentón or smoked paprika
1/8 teaspoon cayenne
3 tablespoons sherry vinegar
1 teaspoon black pepper

1. Slice the potatoes in half. Soak in cold water to release some of the starch; then pat completely dry with paper towels. Lay out in a single layer on a rack-lined baking sheet, uncovered, in the refrigerator for about 30 minutes to get them completely dry.

2. Preheat your grill to medium heat.

3. Add potatoes to a cast-iron skillet; add vegetable oil, salt, and pepper. Turn to coat and spread into a single layer.

4. To begin the romesco sauce, coat tomatoes and bell pepper in 1/2 tablespoon vegetable oil.

5. Cut the head of garlic through the middle horizontally to expose the cloves. Drizzle with 1/2 tablespoon vegetable oil and 1 teaspoon salt; wrap tightly.

6. Add the cast-iron skillet of potatoes to the grill. Along the side of the grill, over indirect heat, add the tomatoes, bell pepper, and foil-wrapped garlic. Close the lid and cook everything for 30 minutes, turning the tomatoes and bell pepper every 10 minutes.

7. After 30 minutes, turn the potatoes. Remove the tomatoes and bell pepper. Check on the garlic; if it is golden and tender, remove it; if not, leave it for the remaining 10–15 minutes.

8. Once the tomatoes and bell pepper have cooled slightly, remove as much of the skins as possible and discard. Cut the bell pepper into large chunks, removing the stem and seeds.

9. Add the tomatoes, bell pepper, 5 cloves of the roasted garlic, 1 1/2 teaspoons salt, and the remaining romesco sauce ingredients to a high-speed blender. Blend on high for about 30 seconds, until completely smooth.

10. After about 45 minutes total cooking time, remove the potatoes. They should be crispy and fork tender. Cooking time may vary, based on the size.

11. Serve the crispy potatoes with a drizzle of romesco sauce and parsley for garnish.

PRO TIPS:

- I cooked these over wood charcoal on my Burch Barrel grill. I was able to control the heat by lowering the lid to just above the top. Make sure your flame is at about a medium heat, the potatoes need time to cook through and become golden brown, so you don't want the heat too high.

- Keep the remaining roasted garlic in the refrigerator to use for sauces, marinades, salad dressings, or even mashed potatoes!

KUNG PAO CAULIFLOWER

This is not your basic cauliflower recipe; it's filled with sweetness and spice and will definitely wake up your taste buds!

1 head cauliflower
1 red bell pepper, stem and seeds removed
3 tablespoons vegetable oil

1 tablespoon torn fresh cilantro, for garnish
1–2 tablespoons peanuts, for garnish

SAUCE

1/3 cup soy sauce
1 tablespoon hoisin sauce
3 tablespoons rice vinegar
1 tablespoon brown sugar
4 scallions, chopped, white and light green parts, reserve dark green parts for garnish
2 cloves of garlic, minced

1/2 tablespoon grated ginger
2 tablespoons spicy chili crisp (or siracha to taste for heat)
2 tablespoons sesame oil
5 dried chiles de árbol
Slurry of 1 cup chicken stock and 1 tablespoon cornstarch

1. Prepare the cauliflower by removing the stem and cutting it into florets.

2. Cut the bell pepper into 1-inch chunks.

3. Preheat the grill to medium heat.

4. Add the cauliflower and bell peppers to a cast-iron pan and toss in vegetable oil. Arrange the vegetables in a single layer on the bottom of the pan. Place on the grill and close the lid. Cook for about 10 minutes.

5. Meanwhile, in a saucepan, combine the sauce ingredients. Bring to a boil and then reduce to a simmer. As soon as it thickens, turn off the heat and set aside.

6. After 10 minutes, turn the cauliflower, browning the other side. Close the lid and cook for another 10 minutes.

7. When the cauliflower is cooked through, drizzle on the sauce and stir to combine. Cook for another 2 minutes and remove.

8. Garnish with the dark green chopped onions, cilantro, and peanuts.

PRO TIPS:

- I love spicy chili crisp; I use it in recipes all the time. If you don't have it, you can substitute siracha, but you may want to start with 1 tablespoon because it can be a little spicier. You can taste it and add more if you want it hotter.

- The dried chiles de árbol in the sauce are there to add spice, but they may be too hot to eat in the dish; feel free to remove them before serving.

GRILLED ELOTE SALAD

Serves 4–6
Prep Time: 10 minutes
Cook Time: 10 minutes
Total Time: 20 minutes

Elote is Mexican street corn on the cob packed with tons of flavors! In this recipe, I have taken all the flavors off the cob and made it easier to eat.

1 jalapeño
8 ears of corn, shucked
2 tablespoons vegetable oil
1/4 red onion, diced

DRY RUB
1/2 tablespoon kosher salt
1/2 tablespoon black pepper
1 teaspoon cumin

DRESSING
1/4 cup sour cream
1 lime, zested and juiced

1/4 cup chopped fresh cilantro, for garnish
4 ounces queso fresco or cotija, crumbled, for garnish

1 teaspoon smoked paprika
1 teaspoon coriander

1 tablespoon chipotle pepper in adobo sauce
1/2 teaspoon kosher salt

1. Preheat the grill to medium heat.

2. In a small bowl, combine the dry rub ingredients.

3. Split the jalapeño in half lengthwise and remove the ribs and seeds.

4. Coat the corn and jalapeño with vegetable oil and sprinkle the dry rub on all sides of the corn.

5. Grill the corn 2–3 minutes per side until some char is achieved. Remove the corn after about 10 total minutes of cooking time.

6. While the corn is grilling, grill the jalapeño for 2 minutes, flip, grill 2 more minutes, and then remove to a platter.

7. Combine the dressing ingredients in a bowl.

8. Cut the corn from the cobs and dice the jalapeño.

9. Add the corn, jalapeño, and onion to the dressing bowl.

10. Stir to combine. Garnish with cilantro and queso fresco or cotija cheese. Serve at room temperature.

ZUCCHINI & SUMMER SQUASH SKEWERS

A great light and tasty side dish all summer long!

This recipe is featured with the Swordfish Skewers with Charred Meyer Lemon Gremolata on page 99.

2 zucchini
2 summer squash
2 tablespoons extra virgin olive oil
2 cloves of garlic, minced
1/2 tablespoon herbes de Provence

1 teaspoon kosher salt
1/2 teaspoon black pepper
Optional garnish: a squeeze of lemon or freshly grated Parmesan cheese

1. Slice zucchini and squash into even slices about 1/2-inch thick.

2. Add zucchini and squash slices to a large bowl and toss with olive oil, garlic, herbes de Provence, salt, and pepper.

3. Skewer vegetables and preheat grill to medium-low, about 325 degrees. Spray grill with non-stick spray.

4. Grill skewers, turning or rotating every 5 minutes after grill marks are achieved and vegetables are tender, about 15 minutes total grilling time.

5. Squeeze with lemon or top with freshly grated Parmesan cheese, if desired.

COCONUT CILANTRO RICE

Serves 4–6
Prep Time: 5 minutes
Cook Time: 20 minutes
Total Time: 25 minutes

This is one of my favorite (and very easy) ways to jazz up plain rice. It adds a sweet contrast to spicy dishes. I love it with Asian dishes, stir-fries, and Thai food!

This recipe is featured with Sweet & Spicy Pork Tenderloin Bowl on page 49.

1 1/2 cups basmati or jasmine rice
1 can (14 ounces) coconut milk
1 teaspoon kosher salt

1/2 cup chicken stock
2 tablespoons chopped fresh cilantro

1. In a pot on the stove over high heat, combine the rice, coconut milk, salt, and chicken stock. Once it starts to boil, reduce immediately to a simmer and cover. Cook for about 20 minutes and then turn off the heat.

2. Before serving, fluff it with a fork and fold in the cilantro.

SMOKED ARTICHOKES

I could eat artichokes all summer long, and I usually do! Steaming them in a broth adds so much more flavor than water alone. Smoking them on the Traeger as a second step gives a touch of wood-fired flavor, and the Artichoke Vinaigrette is a tasty alternative to melted butter or mayo.

3 artichokes
2 cups chicken stock
1 lemon, juiced
1/4 cup white wine
3 cloves of garlic, smashed
2 bay leaves

2 tablespoons extra virgin olive oil
1 teaspoon kosher salt
1/2 teaspoon black pepper
1 lemon, halved
Melted garlic butter, for serving
Mayo, for serving

ARTICHOKE VINAIGRETTE

1 can (8.5 ounces) whole artichoke hearts, drained and rinsed
1/2 lemon, juiced
3 cloves of garlic
1 tablespoon red wine vinegar

1 cup extra virgin olive oil
1 teaspoon kosher salt
1/2 teaspoon black pepper
Water, if desired for thinner consistency

1. Prepare the artichokes by cutting the very top of the artichoke off to make a flat surface. Then cut the stem to leave about 1/2-inch at the base, remove the smaller leaves from around the stem, and use kitchen shears to cut off the pointy edges of each leaf all around the artichoke.

2. In a large dutch oven, add the chicken stock, lemon juice, white wine, garlic, and bay leaves; bring to a boil.

3. Place the artichokes in the simmering liquid top-side down so they sit vertical in the liquid. Reduce to simmer and cover with a lid.

4. Simmer for about 30 minutes until the artichokes are cooked through and the leaves easily pull away. Remove from the pot and allow to cool.

5. Preheat the smoker to 325 degrees.

6. While the artichokes cook, combine the vinaigrette ingredients in a blender. Combine on high until completely smooth. If you prefer a thinner consistency, add a few tablespoons of water until the desired consistency is achieved.

7. Once the artichokes are cooled, carefully cut them in half. This is easiest to do with the top down, cutting directly down the center of the stem. Use a large spoon to scrape out the very inner leaves and the artichoke hair, leaving the rest of the leaves and inner heart intact.

8. In a bowl, mix the artichoke halves with the olive oil, salt, and pepper and then place them on a baking sheet.

9. Smoke them heart-side up for about 30 minutes for some amazing wood-fired flavor. Squeeze half a lemon over the top.

10. Serve the artichokes with Artichoke Vinaigrette, melted garlic butter, or mayo.

BASICS & STAPLES

FIRE-ROASTED SALSA

Prep Time: 20 minutes
Cook Time: 10 minutes
Total Time: 30 minutes

Fire-roasted salsa needs to be added to your chip-and-salsa rotation. Smoking the ingredients brings out so much flavor and makes this a rustic and delicious salsa to enjoy with your Mexican-inspired dishes!

This recipe is featured with Chicken Quesabirria on page 42.

2 large tomatoes, halved
1 jalapeño, sliced in half lengthwise, seeds and ribs removed
1 yellow onion, quartered
2 tablespoons extra virgin olive oil, divided

2 1/2 teaspoons plus a pinch kosher salt, divided
1/2 teaspoon black pepper
5 cloves of garlic
1/2 cup cilantro
1/2 lime, juiced

1. Preheat smoker to 450 degrees.

2. In a large cast-iron pan, add tomatoes, jalapeño, onion, 1 tablespoon olive oil, 1 teaspoon salt, and black pepper; turn to coat.

3. In a foil packet, add garlic, 1 tablespoon olive oil, and a pinch of salt. Close tightly and add the packet to the pan with the other salsa ingredients.

4. Place the cast-iron pan of salsa vegetables in the smoker.

5. After about 30 minutes, flip the salsa vegetables in the pan.

6. When salsa has smoked for 1 hour, remove from smoker. Add the smoked tomatoes, onions, jalapeño, and garlic to a blender. Add cilantro, lime juice, and 1 1/2 teaspoons salt. Blend for about 15 seconds, it will still have some texture. Pour into a bowl, cover, and refrigerate until needed.

ALL-PURPOSE SEASONING

I use this seasoning everywhere, whether I'm cooking inside or outside. It's a great blend that works well on meats, chicken, fish, or vegetables.

This recipe is featured with Smoked BBQ Chicken with Gochujang BBQ Sauce on page 35, Smoked Chicken Enchiladas on page 24, and Grilled Ratatouille on page 111.

2 tablespoons kosher salt
1 tablespoon black pepper
1 tablespoon garlic powder
1 tablespoon onion powder

1 tablespoon paprika
1/2 tablespoon oregano
1 teaspoon celery salt
1/8 teaspoon cayenne

1. Combine all ingredients in a bowl.
2. Can be stored in an airtight container up to one year.

MEXICAN SPICE RUB

Total Time: 5 minutes

This is a go-to rub for all my Mexican-inspired dishes! Once you add the spices to whatever meat you're cooking, you can immediately start to smell the amazing flavors coming out. Store extra in an airtight container for next time!

This recipe is featured with Smoked Pork Chile Verde on page 53.

1 tablespoon kosher salt
1/2 tablespoon black pepper
1 tablespoon cumin
1/2 tablespoon ground coriander
1/2 tablespoon oregano

1 tablespoon garlic powder
1 tablespoon onion powder
1/8 teaspoon cayenne
1 teaspoon smoked paprika

1. Mix all ingredients in a bowl and stir to combine.
2. Use on your favorite cut of meat for Mexican-inspired dishes.

BASIL PESTO

There is nothing better than fresh basil pesto. I love to add it to tomato salads for a pop of summer freshness.

This recipe is featured with Chicken Pesto Pizza on page 40 and Chicken Caprese Sandwiches on page 28.

1/3 cup pine nuts
2 cloves of garlic, roughly chopped
1 teaspoon kosher salt
1 teaspoon black pepper

1 tablespoon lemon juice
2 cups basil leaves
1/2 cup extra virgin olive oil
1/2 cup Parmesan cheese, grated

1. In a blender, combine pine nuts, garlic, salt, pepper, and lemon juice. Pulse to blend.
2. Add the basil leaves and blend.
3. Slowly add olive oil and blend until smooth.
4. Add Parmesan cheese and pulse to combine.
5. Cover the surface of the pesto and the sides of the bowl with plastic wrap to remove any air pockets and prevent browning; refrigerate until ready to use.

TZATZIKI SAUCE

I could eat this sauce alone with a spoon! I add this to all the Greek and Mediterranean dishes I create; the fresh herbs and tangy lemon juice make it a great addition to chicken, pork, and naan.

This recipe is featured with Greek-Inspired Chicken Souvlaki Skewers on page 36.

1 English cucumber
1 cup plain whole milk Greek yogurt
1 tablespoon chopped fresh dill
1 tablespoon chopped fresh oregano
2 cloves of garlic, minced

1/2 lemon, juiced
1 teaspoon kosher salt
1/2 teaspoon black pepper
Drizzle of extra virgin olive oil, for garnish (optional)

1.   Grate the cucumber on a cheese grater over a paper towel, squeeze the grated cucumber in the paper towel over the sink to release as much liquid as possible, and add it to a mixing bowl.

2.   To the mixing bowl, add the yogurt, dill, oregano, garlic, lemon juice, salt, and pepper. Refrigerate until ready to serve and then drizzle with olive oil, if desired.

CRISPY FRIED GARLIC

This is one of my favorite toppings for any Asian-inspired dish—it adds an incredible pop of flavor and texture!

This recipe is featured with Seared Ahi Poke on page 5.

1/2 cup vegetable oil   1 head of garlic, peeled and minced

1. In a large skillet, heat vegetable oil over medium heat.
2. When oil is hot, add the garlic, stirring and turning in the hot oil until just golden brown. It should be done cooking in only 1–2 minutes, watch it, it goes fast!
3. Remove immediately with a slotted spoon and drain on a paper towel-lined plate.

PRO TIP:

- Reserve the garlic oil in the refrigerator for future use in another dish, marinade, or salad dressing.

Total Time: 5 minutes

CHIMICHURRI

Chimichurri on everything! Okay, maybe not everything, but close to it.
It's great on paella, as well as grilled chicken or steak!

This recipe is featured with Arroz con Pollo on page 32.

1 shallot, finely minced
2 cloves of garlic, minced
1/4 cup chopped fresh parsley
1 1/2 tablespoons chopped fresh oregano
1/3 cup chopped fresh cilantro

1/4 teaspoon red pepper flakes
1/4 cup red wine vinegar
1 teaspoon kosher salt
1/2 teaspoon black pepper
3/4 cup extra virgin olive oil

1.   Combine all ingredients in a bowl.

2.   Unused chimichurri can be stored for 1 to 2 weeks in the fridge in an airtight container.

SALSA VERDE

Salsa verde has so much incredible flavor! It adds a lot to other recipes, but it's also good on its own as a salsa with chips!

This recipe is featured with Smoked Pork Chile Verde on page 53.

2 jalapeños, cut in half lengthwise, seeds and ribs removed

2 poblano peppers, cut in half lengthwise, seeds and ribs removed

1 yellow onion, quartered

2 pounds (about 15) tomatillos, rinsed and cut in half

2 tablespoons extra virgin olive oil

4 teaspoons kosher salt, divided

1/2 tablespoon black pepper

2 cloves of garlic, minced

1/2 cup fresh cilantro leaves, stems removed

1 lime, juiced

1. On a sheet pan with edges, line up the jalapeños, poblanos, onion, and tomatillos. Drizzle with olive oil and 1 teaspoon salt.

2. Roast the peppers, onions, and tomatillos on the top rack on a low broil in the oven for about 8 minutes until they start to char. Flip all of them over and broil another 8 minutes. Remove from the oven and allow to cool.

3. Add poblano peppers to a bowl and cover with plastic wrap for 10 minutes. Then, using a paper towel, remove as much of the poblano pepper skin as possible.

4. Add all ingredients from the sheet pan, including the poblanos and all accumulated juices, to a blender. To the blender, also add 3 teaspoons salt and pepper, garlic, cilantro, and lime juice. Blend on high speed for about 30 seconds until completely smooth.

PRO TIP:

- As an alternative, you can also smoke the ingredients for the salsa verde. Place the jalapeño and poblano peppers, onions, and tomatillos on a baking sheet and drizzle with olive oil, salt, and pepper. Smoke at 425 degrees for 10 minutes, flip, and smoke another 10 minutes. Pour the ingredients, along with accumulated juices, into the blender to blend with garlic, cilantro, and lime juice.

PICKLED RED ONIONS

These Pickled Red Onions are perfect any time you want a crunchy, acidic bite to wake up your taste buds. I always make a big batch of an entire red onion and store it in an airtight container for the next few days to use on salads or tacos.

This recipe is featured with Arroz con Pollo on page 32.

1 tablespoon white sugar
1 tablespoon kosher salt
1/2 cup apple cider vinegar
1/4 cup hot water

5 whole peppercorns
1 bay leaf
1 red onion, thinly sliced

1. In a medium bowl, add the sugar, salt, apple cider vinegar, hot water, peppercorns, and bay leaf. Stir until the hot water has blended the salt and sugar with the other ingredients.

2. Add the onion to the bowl, stir to coat, and refrigerate until needed. If onions are not covered in the liquid, add a little more water to cover.

BASIL VINAIGRETTE

A variation on a vinaigrette with the addition of fresh basil to brighten up your dish! This can be used on grilled vegetables, in a salad, or with chicken, shrimp, or pasta, just to name a few ideas.

This recipe is featured with Grilled Ratatouille on page 111.

1/2 cup extra virgin olive oil
2 cups packed fresh basil
2 cloves of garlic
3 tablespoons red wine vinegar

1 teaspoon kosher salt
1/2 teaspoon black pepper
1 teaspoon dijon mustard

1. Combine all ingredients in a blender on high until blended and completely smooth.
2. Store in an airtight container in the fridge for up to a week.

PINEAPPLE SALSA

This Pineapple Salsa is great on tacos, especially chicken, pork, or fish.

This recipe is featured with Kalua Pork Quesadillas on page 61 and Mahi Mahi Tacos on page 96.

2 cups pineapple, diced
1 jalapeño, diced, seeds and ribs removed (leave them in for more spice)
1/2 cup red onion, diced

1/4 cup chopped fresh cilantro
1/2 lime, juiced
1 teaspoon kosher salt
1/2 teaspoon black pepper

1. In a bowl, combine all ingredients.
2. Cover and refrigerate until ready to serve.

Total Time: 5 minutes

MANGO SALSA

This Mango Salsa is perfect on grilled pork, chicken, or seafood. It can even be added to a summer salad. The key is to be sure the mango is very ripe so it's perfectly sweet!

This recipe is featured with Apple Cider Brined Pork Tenderloin on page 61.

1 mango, peeled and diced
1 jalapeño, diced, seeds and ribs removed
1/4 red onion, diced
1/4 cup chopped fresh cilantro

1/2 lime, juiced
1/2 teaspoon kosher salt
1/4 teaspoon black pepper
1 tablespoon extra virgin olive oil

1.   Combine all ingredients in a bowl.
2.   Cover and place in the refrigerator until ready to serve.

GOCHUJANG BBQ SAUCE

The instant I created this Gochujang BBQ Sauce as a variation from the original, my family fell in love! The flavors work incredibly well, and the gochujang adds a great sweet-heat umami flavor.

This recipe is featured with Smoked BBQ Chicken on page 35.

1 1/2 cups ketchup
1/2 cup gochujang
3/4 cup apple cider vinegar
1 cup water, more as needed while it reduces
1/2 cup light brown sugar
1 tablespoon onion powder

1 tablespoon garlic powder
1 teaspoon ground mustard
2 tablespoons Worcestershire sauce
1 teaspoon black pepper
Squeeze of lemon

1. Combine all ingredients in a saucepan on the stove.
2. Simmer on low for 1 hour.

PRO TIPS:

- Stir sauce occasionally. If it is reducing too quickly, add another 1/2 cup water as needed.
- For a classic BBQ sauce, simply omit the gochujang and add another 1/2 cup ketchup (for a total of 2 cups).
- Any unused sauce can be stored in an airtight container in the fridge for 1 to 2 weeks.

HOMEMADE MARINARA

Prep Time: 5 minutes
Cook Time: 1 hour, 15 minutes
Total Time: 1 hour, 20 minutes

Everyone needs a homemade marinara recipe you can make with your eyes closed. It's so easy and so delicious and fresh tasting!

This recipe is featured with Roasted Tomato, Pesto & Shrimp Crostini on page 13, Garlic Butter Monkey Bread with Marinara on page 9, and Smoked Meatballs on page 70.

2 tablespoons extra virgin olive oil
1 yellow onion, diced
5 cloves of garlic, minced
1 tablespoon kosher salt
1 teaspoon black pepper
1 teaspoon dried Italian seasoning
1/2 teaspoon red pepper flakes
2 tablespoons tomato paste

1 cup red wine
2 cans (28 ounces each) crushed San Marzano
    tomatoes
1 cup water
2 bay leaves
2 tablespoons chopped fresh parsley
2 tablespoons chopped fresh basil
1/2 tablespoon granulated sugar

1. Heat a large Dutch oven to medium heat. Add olive oil and onions and sauté until soft and translucent, but not browned, about 10 minutes.

2. Add garlic and cook 1 more minute. Add salt, pepper, Italian seasoning, red pepper flakes, and tomato paste; stir to combine and cook for 5 minutes.

3. Add red wine, bring to a boil, and then reduce to a simmer.

4. Add tomatoes and then use water to rinse both cans and get out the remaining tomatoes. Add the tomato-water to the sauce.

5. Add bay leaves, parsley, basil, and sugar. Stir to combine and simmer for at least 1 hour. If simmering for longer, add more water as needed as sauce reduces.

ABOUT FAMILIUS

VISIT OUR WEBSITE: WWW.FAMILIUS.COM

Familius is a global trade publishing company that publishes books and other content to help families be happy. We believe that happy families are key to a better society and the foundation of a happy life. The greatest work anyone will ever do will be within the walls of his or her own home. And we don't mean vacuuming! We recognize that every family looks different and passionately believe in helping all families find greater joy, whatever their situation. To that end, we publish beautiful books that help families live our 10 Habits of Happy Family Life: *love together, play together, learn together, work together, talk together, heal together, read together, eat together, give together,* and *laugh together.* Further, Familius does not discriminate on the basis of race, color, religion, gender, age, nationality, disability, caste, or sexual orientation in any of its activities or operations. Founded in 2012, Familius is located in Sanger, California.

CONNECT

Facebook: www.facebook.com/familiusbooks
Pinterest: www.pinterest.com/familiusbooks
Instagram: @FamiliusBooks
TikTok: @FamiliusBooks

The most important work you ever do will be within the walls of your own home.